[handwritten inscription] ... Be ... about the value of what you USP is? Best, *[signature]*

MORE
BALLS
THAN
MOST

MORE
BALLS
THAN
MOST

**Juggle your way to
success with proven
company shortcuts**

Lara Morgan

First published in 2011 by
Infinite Ideas Limited
36 St Giles
Oxford
OX1 3LD
United Kingdom
www.infideas.com

A CIP catalogue record for this book is available from the British Library

ISBN 978-1-906821-73-9

Brand and product names are trademarks or registered trademarks of their respective owners.

Cover designed by Darren Hayball
Cover photograph by Pete Corbin at www.fovea.tv
Text designed and typeset by Nicki Averill
Printed and bound in Great Britain

This book is dedicated to my family, but above all to my husband Charlie, without whom the journey would not have been half as much fun.

To my mum and dad, who influenced my appreciation of the importance of education, culture and hard work.

To my brother, Alec, whose competitive presence has ensured that I have remained focused.

Contents

Acknowledgements

My never-ending thanks
to all those who have aided, abetted
and encouraged me. The importance of the
Pacific team, and our friends and suppliers, cannot
be expressed more highly: priceless people, who placed
priceless faith in me and my company.

It was a no-brainer to value my team, the people I depended
on, those who took the risk to work with me; they came first in
everything we did. They paid me back in the most extraordinary
ways. Not only with immense loyalty, striving to go the extra
mile, with endless care for continual improvement – but also
with care for individuals of all moods and positions within
the company. The opportunity to share international
experiences, learn about new cultures and travel to
foreign lands was a pearl afforded by the 24/7
hospitality industry, for which I have the
deepest level of respect. I could not
have been luckier than to work in
and serve an industry full of like-
minded players who continually
put their faith in our service.

The infectiously positive culture
safeguarded by those
who arrived early gave
us advantage beyond
all others, and I miss
working with them all:

Rachel
Groom, Margaret and
Robert Oakley, David Groom, Caroline
Godfrey (Keen Shay Keens), David and Sue Brown
(Buckingham Soap), Brian Woodrow, Gillian Smith, Carol
Fake, Oliver Bennett, Mandy Brooks, Sarah King, Lisa Graves,
Parveen Mahay, Bedford Hockey Club, Richard O'Connell, Louise
Guard, Carolyn Norman, Stephen Oliver (Woodfines Solicitors),
Wille Grongvist (Teampac), Dawn Eaton, Stuart Johnston, Peter Bell
(Bradford Soaps), Fay Pottinger, Maurizio Beretta, Ben Fong, Richard
Lam, Yan Yong, Claire Timms, David Murgatroyd, Lisa Pywell, Carl
Hooley, Jim Johnston, Tim Allen (Flame Solutions), Robert Dupree,
Kate Parkin and the Parkin family, Colin Barrow, Travor Pasquire
(HSBC), Nigel Alldritt, Tim Leach, Penny Ferguson, Fran Saunders,
Nicki Tallentire, Nita Sinclair, Diana Smolka, Pauline Watkins,
Maria di Paolo, Neil Fake, Deborah Hartley, Nino Silvestri,
Mandy Parker, Faye Klein, Jo Hakewill, Barbara Auton,
Janice Blackett, Sue Lowe, Claire Hyde, Deborah
Jones, Jeremy Taylor, Dawn Eaton, Richard
Percival, Andrew Botting, Tom Fairhurst,
Ashley Meddings, Dan Ellison, Denise
Hooper, Hayley Ward, Becky Coster,
Marianne Janse Van Rensburg,
Simon Powell, Barbara Auten,
Trish Marshall, Roberto Barbato,
Donna Rankin, Julia Palmer,
Jeremy Taylor, Stephan
Heldt, Helen Burnage,
Abby Summerville,
Rachel Hurren, Kristie
McPherson, Carol Ann
Sleap, Albie Mottershaw,
Sandra Miles,

Janice Peace,
Abi Crowley, Daniel Smith,
Wendy Kemp, Dawn Davies, Paola Reid,
Barry Stuart, Shacy Lim, Susan Terry, Stephanie
Currer, Ian Morris (lawyer, EMW Picton Howell).

From International: Martin Samek, Oliver Hromek, Marketa
Kopecka, Jana Kmentova, Alena Brandova, Peter Tropp, Peter
Kulharrvy, Joseph Tesarik, Michaela Klinger, Simon and Irene
Cheung, Serina Vong, Francis Yang, Vicki Lam, Angus Hung, and in
the USA, Patrick Gallagher, Bill Wilson and John Gallagher.

And from licensing friends, customer friends – and some great
brands: Vicki Laws, Jayne Walton (Jarvis Hotels), Melanie
Walmsley (Forte Hotels), David Elder (Alliance National),
Sean Harrington (Elemis), Oriele Frank (Elemis), Michelle
Smith (Penhaligons), Michael Sweeney (Natural
Products World), Aveda, Floris, The White
Company, Ermeneguildo Zegna, Bulgari,
Asprey, and many more superb brand
creators and owners, all of whom I
am proud to have represented.

I would also like to acknowledge the
help I have received from HSBC,
Dale Carnegie, Cranfield Business
Growth   Development
Programme and Stanford
University, USA.

Introduction

The story of the growth of my company Pacific Direct – the globally recognised supplier and manufacturer of retail-branded guest amenities to world-renowned hotels – is clearly precious to me.

I founded Pacific Direct with almost nothing and sold it for £20 million. I hope that sharing the trials and tribulations of my past business failures and my ultimate success will allow others to believe in themselves, persevere as they overcome hurdles and obstacles, and enable those who have the right state of mind to create their own success.

I have worked outrageously hard. I have made more mistakes than I dare to admit and I have by no means been perfect in my treatment of people. I'm a jack of all trades and master of one: I am horribly proud to boast about being a world-class sales person. There is no such thing as a business without a purchase order; there is no need for any systems or processes whatsoever until an order comes in.

Business is not a game, although it remains relentlessly competitive. Without being brutally honest with yourself first and foremost, you will never maximise small business growth potential. Knowing where you stand with cash and finance is business critical. You will have to make horrible decisions as you grow – decisions which at the time will seem huge but which, in hindsight, will be only a few of the myriad of difficult decisions you will have to make in order to progress. See everything as a possible opportunity and remain open-minded to change and challenges. Learn continually, find time to 'smell the coffee' – though don't drink too much of it – and please, please, *please* have a plan. I wish that I had thought more deeply and planned with much better focus at an earlier phase. I will never know whether this approach would have paid dividends, but as my business grew I did start to spend quality time on thinking through, working out and devising clear steps for achieving goals. My initial goals, simplistic as they sound, were to pay the bills, make a bit of money and have a job to do – all of which were driven by the fear of failure.

Expect change, accept correction, admit that you might sometimes be wrong. Do not do what you have always done, or be sure that you can be content with getting what you have always got. Irrespective of anything, unless you apply change and learning you will bobble along in the turbulent and sometimes less-rewarding world of small business without ever realising your full potential. The harder you work, the more opportunities you will create. It is selecting the best and most profitable opportunities, those that are able to be repeatedly sold, and sold with little impact on administration, that could accelerate profitable fast growth. In working 'hard and smart' you will create your own luck. By being in touch with the customer, listening to feedback and by being in the right place at the right time connections are inevitably made that – when followed through – lead to profitable outcomes. Things happen because people act. Too many times people promise to follow up or make contact following an event and then fail to do so. Action does indeed favour the brave, and a significant reason for writing this book is to thank those people who 'went with the whirlwind'.

So the objective of this book is to share the roller-coaster journey of conscious incompetence and small company growth possibilities with other leaders in the hope of inspiring staying power, underlining the power of learning and focus and, I hope, also injecting fun, flexibility and celebration into organisations around the world. But, whilst remaining down-to-earth and working your backside off, do not forget the importance of actually enjoying the journey.

Read on, enjoy, laugh and cry – but whatever you do, do not forget to apply the suggestions I make in this book to your own business.

1

Success is for idiots

Chapter goals

- Limited foundations are required – and next to no plan.
- Have a product to sell with an unrefined strategy – evolve as you go.
- Apply lessons from life.
- Respect people and money – budget from the outset and employ the best you can afford.

Pacific Direct, my business, was launched in 1991 on the steps of the Dorchester (this might be over-egging it somewhat, as the Dorchester was closed at the time for a massive refurbishment). This was literally the place where I pulled my shoulders back, stood up straight and steeled myself for my first hotel amenities sales meeting. I had arrived, care of the Tube, and found myself effectively on the Monopoly board – standing on the really expensive blue bit of Park Lane, in one of the wealthiest parts of London. I was as nervous as hell, a little sick with anticipation and shaking at the knees.

My appointment was in a less glamorous office nearby. In my bag I had a sample of a brand new and unique sewing kit – unique because the needles were already threaded – and barely anything else other than old and inelegant sample products with Chinese printing on them.

I was ushered into a room and brought out my wares. The Purchasing Manager was amazed; he'd never seen one of these sewing kits before. He asked for a quote for 10,000 – that was a year's supply. 'Fantastic,' I thought. 'My first sale. Easy business this.'

Then, as I left, the Purchasing Manager said to me, 'You will store these for us in England, deliver within twenty-four hours, we only pay for the ones that we have delivered, they'll be customised with the name "The Dorchester", and we'll expect you to hold stock. You do have a warehouse, don't you?'

'Absolutely,' I said. 'Not a problem. All as I expected.' I was somewhat stretching the bounds of reality here. Unless you counted the space under my desk and my fax machine under the stairs, I had no warehouse, no delivery system and no brochure. But I did have a determination – you might even call it a strategy, a simple one really: sell stuff, make a profit and then repeat the process.

Little did I know then the power and importance of selling to one of the world's most prestigious properties. The value of being able to quote the Dorchester as my first client was critical and became very much the core introduction of every cold call I made thereafter. I quickly realised this, and have used the focus of winning a well-recognised, prestigious account as a door-opener all over the world since, but at that moment I had a lot to learn. Although I knew a bit about designing and customising products from my first full-time sales job in Hong Kong selling promotional giveaway items, back then I'd had the back-up of a team of designers. However, at Marlow Promotions I had actually learnt far more than I had realised. Learning to source products direct from Chinese manufacturers, have them made in a client's brand colours and printed with a big-brand message, and then having them packaged and delivered according to client demand was an asset that repeatedly gave me great foundations for what was, at that time, yet to come.

I should add at this point that this was the first step in Pacific's strategy, even though it took me a long time until I realised that it was indeed a strategy. I made the appointment at the Dorchester because my grandmother had talked about parties in London in her youth. She had mentioned the likes of the Savoy and the Dorchester and had described dancing in the Strand at New Year. I will never forget her saying that if I was determined to sell to hotels, then she advised me to sell to only the very best. The sheer luck of winning my first business and having somewhere like the Dorchester as my very first customer opened nearly every other hotel door in the world as a new opportunity.

I was most certainly a one-man band in the UK, and this was a completely new ball game. I had three months to deliver the order. I knew I had to learn, and fast. So I did what I always do. I behaved like an idiot – and I started listening a lot and asking lots of questions.

My background

My father wanted to be a millionaire by the age of 40; instead he declared bankruptcy the year I left school. One consequence of this is that I have no qualifications past A level, but I have no regrets about attending the 'university of life'. I was born in Germany and pretty much immediately moved to Hong Kong with my family. My father was then in the army but handed in his commission and took a role with ICL. He left to set up his own company in computer software development in the late 1970s, which apparently failed because he ran out of cash. I think I now understand why this happened; he was a middleman hardware provider as well as a software designer, and did not react to the changing marketplace as the demand for computers took off. Agents for the big brands became redundant as the companies changed tack and took their products direct to the marketplace. All in all, it was a difficult time.

So why do I believe that I had a wonderful upbringing, as I do? Well, throughout the turmoil I had a very normal and happy childhood. At the time, being short of money was just part of how my brother and I planned what we did. We managed to have the guts to scrounge lifts, instead of paying for transport; the odd jobs we did bolstered our meagre income. And experience gained from cleaning out sheds for my uncle or working in market research for my aunt gave me the skills which I successfully applied during the development of Pacific Direct. Our parents taught us to respect our belongings and used the performance of the business to explain why we always had to be careful with money. They also brought us up with values which have stayed with me and influence how I have approached everything, and I picked up two vital principles at school: firstly, always do your best and secondly, the more you put into something, the more you will get out.

The extraordinary contrasts of my childhood – for example, being sent to boarding school and then, as my parents steadily ran out of money, having to spend the holidays with relatives where I would have to work to earn pocket money – meant that I grew up determined to have enough money to live my life with choice. My underlying determination for success was based on my own childhood experiences and ultimately my absolute bottom line was being able to afford the life I chose. I did not see money as the be all and end all, but it bought what I wanted: security. As I matured and became a parent myself, it bought for my children the great gift my parents worked so relentlessly to afford for us – the best education they could buy. If you are untargeted and aimless, how will you know how to maximise your potential?

Back to Park Lane

So imagine yourself (unqualified other than with some sales experience), at the age of 23, standing for the first time on the steps of one of the world's most famous and glamorous hotels on London's Park Lane.

I'd just started a company in a country I had never lived in because I basically needed a job, and 1991 was the middle of a recession – something I knew nothing about. I had been given the opportunity to make some money selling hotel accessories by two gentlemen who had been shareholders of a company I had previously worked for in Hong Kong. They had recently purchased a factory making such accessories and were struggling to control the production of orders which were coming in from around the world. Actually, they did not really have a full hotel amenities range; they did sewing kits, some shoe polishers and shower caps; no soap, only soap dishes, and toiletry bottles which looked as though they had been designed in the dark ages.

My job was to sell these items to hotels in the UK as the representative of the factory in China. At the time I thought it was in no way odd to print 'Factory Representative' on my name card – I had grown up in the world of China trading and thought everyone knew that China was where labour-intensive manufactured goods came from. To my surprise this was not indeed the case, and it seemed that my very global view of the world was much more the exception than the rule.

The little I knew then about soaps and toiletries was matched only by the little I knew about hotels in Britain. Although I'd passed through London before, I'd only ever emerged from the Tube at the railway station or airport. But I had got my order. So I rang up freight companies and asked how the freight system worked. I spoke to people who ran warehouses, I found designers who dealt in artwork. As the kits were coming from Hong Kong, I spoke to people in imports to find out how to get them through customs and into the UK. When I picked up the phone to these people, the words I used then, and still use today (like a mantra, my staff tell me), were 'Treat me like an idiot, because I know nothing'. I'm always amazed at how few other people in business do the same thing.

I was nervous and certainly in uncharted territory, but I'd had a highly successful career in sales in Hong Kong, the Gulf States and New Zealand. I somehow had the confidence that the selling part of this new business wasn't going to be too difficult. I did not have the encumbrance of too much experience (and I admire all the more those people who set up companies later in life when they have far more at risk). I saw 'the rest of business' as the application of processes using common sense, having the intelligence – I would call it nous – to ask and not being embarrassed about not knowing things. Most importantly, I had the determination to work hard and the spirit and state of mind to never give up.

Know what you don't know, and apply what you have learnt

The only focus I had in those very early days was the need to pay my bills. It was automatic for me to need to know the break-even figure and the point at which I made money each month. I had no company vision for success, no goals, no annual objectives. I did have a desk, all the hours in the day and my health – and never undervalue the importance of having your health. One of the first things I knew I had to learn about was accounting and, in my simple language, 'where's the money?' Back in those early days, I didn't have the income to employ anyone else. For two years, I did all the cold calling, bin emptying, selling, and often the delivering too. I was also running the business, right down to doing the accounts – only I knew next to nothing about accounts.

My upbringing had enabled me to recognise how critical money was and what effect it can have on your freedom. At 18, I had borrowed my first business clothes and gone for an interview. From day one of my very first job I imposed a savings plan on myself – spending 10 per cent of my commissions and never exceeding my base salary income in expenditure. That decision alone gave me the capital with which to establish my own company later, and do so without any borrowing. I started to amass some quite considerable savings as my commissions grew rapidly – in fact, they grew to the point where the company I worked for adjusted the commission scheme to reduce my earnings. The experience of that unfair decision was a powerful one, and the memory of it ensured that I always tried to focus on the fair treatment of the people I employed and had a consistent approach when it came to terms. I actually managed to cover my living costs for the whole of the first year of Pacific Direct thanks to the £17,000 in savings that I accumulated.

Learning to sell

If there is one thing that I can do (and I would hope to a good level), it is sell. I enjoy the process of relationship building; I would like to think I have practised selling – also referred to as 'rainmaking' – as an art form. I would also like to think I listened to the customer really well. I know this is really the secret to successful selling but it is something I still have to practise relentlessly, and which I still get wrong.

Selling is like a funnel. It's about effort at the top and pushing stuff through to the bottom, converting orders of different shapes and sizes in a continual flow. But it is not simply about being busy with opportunities; it is about filling the funnel with high-quality, strategic fit, profitable opportunities. I always equated this effort with a competitive race of some kind and have always felt that even if I was not the best at selling, I would succeed if I could put in more effort, do so in a better way than other people and juggle more balls than most. My effort has always been repaid in some shape or form and I advocate that approach still. Many people think they work hard, when they're not actually making the sacrifices necessary to fill the funnel and fill it relentlessly. If you do not continually focus on opportunity creation your business will hiccup and fly forward a bit like an old banger filled with kangaroo petrol. This is difficult for all sorts of reasons. It is much more stressful than a continual flow, and it's also easier said than done. I learnt to sell without any formal training until my work experience in Bell Canada Yellow Pages, Bahrain. The training of the 'steps of the sale' process is without question the smartest sales lesson I had experienced and I have used the same techniques of understanding the sales step progression progress ever since – you will find a lot more explanation in chapter 3. I love selling and feel that most business success stems from someone who can sell.

Selling requires passion, honesty and integrity and energy like few other roles in business. In return for hard work I have had bags of wonderful experiences, met a wide range of people in a huge number of countries and sometimes even squealed with joy in my most successful moments.

The development of hearing customer needs (and sometimes customer wants) is only a very early stage in the sales process. Fact-finding missions result in work creation, possibly in product sourcing, development, costings and price setting. You aim to return to a customer with an irresistible offer presented in a professional and timely manner. You will then start to encounter rejection and hurdles, and over the years I have experienced all kinds of procrastination and delays. Selling is not by any means about price alone. If you can learn from the earliest stage that the value of meeting a client's needs is the most important objective (obviously with new solutions it is also about education), and that this is often not price first, you will be wholly more successful. You will have more selling time for more sales to others – or more sales to the same opportunity, which can be even better.

The importance of cash

Cranfield School of Management reports, following extensive study, that most small companies go out of business because they don't manage their money – the figure is around 51 per cent in the first five years after start up. I wasn't prepared to let the same thing happen to me. I knew that I needed to manage the money from day one; I just had to find someone to help me do it.

A religious approach to cash will also be required in your company as it was in mine. In the early days I looked at the cash in our bank account every day; I would always know what was owing and what was due, and I controlled the cash to the point of filling in my own VAT return for the first three years. In a small start-up company I cannot recommend more highly the power of making your own computer or pencilled entries. Bought ledger, sales ledger and controlling accounts all the way through to the first cheque I wrote for HMRC remains with me and has stood me in good stead. Take very seriously indeed the saying that turnover is vanity, profit is sanity and cash is reality. Then continue to take this point seriously all the way through the management of your company and all the way through to exit, should you so choose. Cash in your bank is the final measure of your success if you have chosen exit as your measure.

I needed to find the best person that I could to teach me all about accounting practice. I applied a self-imposed rule of averages, with three being the minimum. This is like my own tendering system, and I have applied it continuously. I called three local accountants, explained who I was and what I wanted and asked if they would teach me how to do my own books. Those who said, 'By all means, come in and have a talk and we'll see what we can do' were my kind of people and got lots of points; in the case of people you are going to work with, always meet face to face before making final decisions. I decided which one I liked more, which I thought was the most competent, which understood me most – and which one was willing to put up with an idiot, because that's what I was. (Today I would take references, ask more detailed track-record questions and be far more rigorous in my interview technique.)

Asking is the fast route to profit

I'm continually surprised at how many businesses are run off a naive 'we will work it out' attitude without putting in the real effort to overcome obstacles. It disappoints me to see so many people with so little dynamism, passion and gumption – or, more importantly, who are so lacking in self-confidence. To state the obvious, bags of self-confidence are required in setting up and running a business. The faster you apply that confidence, the faster you will accumulate profit.

It's amazing – priceless in my opinion – the advantage which businesses can gain if their people just ask those with more knowledge and experience rather than pretending that they know everything. There are a lot of people in this world who want to go directly from A to B but they're terrified to ask directions for how to get there. I ask and ask, and I keep asking. Yes, be memorable, be different, be self-confident and committed – I believe it's better to be remembered (politely) than to have never made an impression at all – but I hope that on my gravestone someone will print the words, 'If you don't ask, you don't get'. This gumption and lack of fear of a little embarrassment – or perhaps the endless practice I have put into overcoming the fact that I've made a fool of myself – have enabled me to speed up all sorts of demands, not least asking directions to somewhere. In business the ability to ask experts is priceless. Often those around you have exactly the answer you are looking for – so don't delay, ask.

In my view, getting a literal head start is vital in business. When I started Pacific Direct, I used to pack all my sewing kits into my car earlier than the crack of dawn, shoot down to London from Bedford, and make all my own deliveries almost before my competitors were out of bed. I'd be delivering kits to the back of the Dorchester at the same time as the kitchens were taking in the fresh fish. That early start meant I beat the traffic and by the time the competition got to their desks, I was on my first selling appointment of the day. I'd used my time as efficiently and effectively as possible, and I had that precious head start. I'm every bit as much a believer in the value of this tactic today.

Standing still is not an option if speed is what you want, as other businesses are already overtaking you in the race to succeed. In fact, constantly living in the fear that others are overtaking should keep you on your toes, so stop messing about and have a go. For me, time is money. If I need a piece of information I think about how I'm going to get what I need as quickly as possible and I go for it. I'm going to do it in the most effective and efficient way, irrespective of pride. And if I believe that the most effective and efficient way is to be humble enough to say 'show me' or 'tell me how', then I will do that.

You need to do something and you can't afford to wait around, so just do it. The personal triumph comes in the rewards of what you learn along the way. Yes, sometimes mistakes are made, but nine times out of ten you hold the advantage because knowledge is power. Knowledge, like money, doesn't grow on trees.

Ask and you'll learn something

The other huge advantage asking gives you is that you'll educate yourself in the process. You'll find out something you didn't know, and you should constantly be learning as much as you can about your own business. You might feel apprehensive about ringing up a stranger and asking for help but, as long as you're learning, that apprehension very quickly fades into the background. Each day you become more knowledgeable and more experienced, and then you can make better judgements. Equally, what once seemed to be massive hurdles are now more like the insignificant, ordinary trials of the day. So the next time you're faced with a similar problem you know what to do.

In this process of learning you're putting yourself more in control of your own business, and you're challenging yourself, taking yourself out of your comfort zone. One of the reasons Pacific Direct developed a hugely successful team and company culture was, I think, because I challenged people to stretch themselves all the time. During breaks we discussed the challenges and opportunities of the day and shared learning. Individuals across all facets of the company would be asked to stand up, move to the front of the room and present their progress – and gradually the whole team could stand and talk to anyone in public.

And this brings me to the key quality you need to have when you're asking for help. It's not the courage to pick up the phone and ask the question. It's humility: the humility to be able to admit that you don't know it all. A priceless ability to swallow your pride and want to learn combined with a determined desire to go places will take you far. Drive is 'the' thing, but humility in behaviour will be well received and always repaid in volume. I think some of the greatest business people are those where you have no idea how amazing an organisation they run because they're humble. You can be demanding whilst being respectful; you can be direct whilst being fair and consistent. Believe every person has something to offer and you will not go far wrong. Give trust first and rarely will that trust be abused.

When I've got the approach right I cannot remember an occasion when someone has said 'I'm not prepared to help you.' In general, people don't drive to work thinking they're going to deliberately annoy those they encounter during the day; almost all people are willing to educate and teach others. Always look to be progressive and challenging and allow your team to step up in the same way as you drive yourself. Failure comes from those who do not build momentum all around them. A classic example is the small business owner whose business fails because he or she is too controlling and unable to build solid, trusted and talented players across the business. So ask. Think about it from the other person's point of view. If somebody says to you, 'Treat me like an idiot', you know that person is being open and genuine. As long as you approach people in the right way – in a humble, gracious, interested, enthusiastic and respectful manner – then you can have anything.

That's why this is my first principle. It underlies so many things vital to any business: fast growth, knowledge, control and power. Behave like an idiot and you really will get the world. Think about it. Start out by making someone smile and relax, compliment their experience and show an interest, and they'll be eating out of your hands before you know it. How could they not help?

Lara's laws

- Get the show on the road with the basics and work out the rest as you progress – orders make for business, plans are nothing without sales.
- Know what you don't know; ask often, refine and apply your logic, and trust in your gut feeling.
- Ask with humility and you'll always learn something; the less you talk, the more you will learn.
- Ask nicely – just because you run the business doesn't mean you know it all.

2

Shut up and listen – it's all about the people

Chapter goals

- Be yourself – leading by example is critical.
- Build and work on the culture of your business.
- Unorthodox recruitment methods can pay great dividends.

People are critical to success, and that's people both inside and outside the company. Your team have much more to give you than you could possibly give them. If you can break down the barriers of hierarchy, be approachable and consistent and persuade them relentlessly to play as team contributors – utilising great ideas and celebrating them as coming from someone within the team – then you will harness power and succeed much faster.

During the early years of Pacific's development, from 1993 to1996, a great deal was achieved. We moved from the front room of a flat to the first floor of a house I bought in a residential area of Bedford. We grew to have six members of staff and had a main supplier from China manufacturing our amenities. I had the brains to employ the bookkeeper who had been doing our books as a subcontractor, and she joined us full time. We even automated our accounts, and elected to go with Sage, then an up-and-coming package that appeared to meet our needs. A good accounting platform gives you both confidence and freedom because it means you have straightforward tax returns, no pay-roll headaches and you can focus on your business.

At this point I attended a Dale Carnegie course on leadership skills. Here I learnt the difference between different styles of management – or perhaps I gained value in recognising that I was doing naturally what good leaders do. Not perfectly, but I did have the chance to compare my skills with others on the course and was delighted to find I could hold my own. And it was an evening course, which was perfect – there was no disruption of the sales day. To my delight I found that I had some natural planning abilities as well as a somewhat rough vision of success. I wrote my 'should be' plan as opposed to thinking about the 'as is' (meaning how things were) and started to visualise where I would take the business next. By this time I was already running the business according to a plan; I'd needed to write one as I had, well before this time, needed to convince a bank to lend me funding.

We were working in an open-plan office, otherwise known as the living room of my home. We used to have lunch around the kitchen table and continually shared client information, celebrated successful sales and built a relentless momentum from our positive and continued successes. We developed new product ranges ourselves and had a ball inventing new products; you don't have to pay creatives in order to be creative. (Romanesque, for example, was designed with the sole purpose of being different from everything else in the marketplace. There were peach and pearl-coloured designs with a picture of a Roman baths.) The determination always to be 'better and different' remained the backbone of our intentions throughout my years at Pacific.

We won our first really major hotel chain in 1993 with Jarvis Hotels, and then with a stroke of luck they more than doubled in size – and so did our sales to them. We had started to create quite a noise amongst the housekeeping fraternity in the UK. We used to take any and every opportunity to meet people, expose our brand and products and to sell. In those days we were a very different company, with the biggest proportion of our goods being custom- or tailor-made products. It was only after a while that we had enough cash to invent our own designed 'house brand' which was available to sell to any hotel. And at some stage during our long and excellent relationship with Jarvis Hotels, we did create their own look and brand of toiletries.

A strong culture in a business is not created overnight, but the foundations of your leadership style will impact very heavily on how others in your company behave around you. You laugh and others will laugh with you. You share mistakes and talk openly about results, encouraging a lack of hierarchy, and other people will appreciate this approach and steadily buy into those values. You cannot buy culture – you have to create it, engender it and nurture the mood of the business. I cannot underline enough the value of honest, open communication about everything in performance terms. As Pacific Direct grew, I shared every month whether we lost or gained money, how much we'd lost or gained and what margins we were making. I think the fact that we set out to share our performance and our challenges helped us immeasurably towards achieving our goals. There is nothing wrong with being obsessed with results, but how you go about sharing these is important to bringing others with you on your journey.

If you are setting up in a business as a new player and have decided to establish yourself because you believe there is a gap in the market – a niche opportunity – then make sure you communicate it clearly and succinctly all the time, from the outset. Just as importantly, and at whatever stage, continually check and make sure your representatives, colleagues and team are utterly clear on the exact mission and service that the business offers. The same critical point must be applied to the way you and your team answer the telephone.

Spend more time listening and encouraging than telling. Wise customers, well-networked suppliers and even the competition can be a massive source of ideas, information and industry trends you need to know about. Your meetings with people do not always need to be formalised. Indeed, it is important to continually shake up your routine to keep things fresh in every aspect of what you do. Have you ever simply dropped in on a good customer with a bunch of flowers as thanks? Small gifts go a long way.

Respect each other's time – and communicate

The stress of time and interruptions in every business becomes a hot topic as staff become pushed and the business grows at an accelerated rate. It's not always easy. We wore baseball caps as a 'do not disturb sign', tried putting different articles on the tops of computer monitors to show that people should not be interrupted, and even set up a space where anyone could work on a computer in peace.

When it comes to meetings, we developed two system templates, and you can find copies for download on www. companyshortcuts.com/documents. If a meeting is called formally and numerous guests (internal or external) are invited, then please, please, please, apply the templates. They will help maximise the results of the meeting, and invariably maximise the value of your business in the process.

You need to develop within your business a culture of continual learning, open communication lines, trust and the will to succeed – or, in other words, 'do as you would be done by'. My determination not to fail was the base around which we built a continual need for progression, improvement and business development.

It was important that everyone in our company knew, understood and drove towards the company goals. Over the years we used process maps, pictures, music, video, toys (a blow-up global ball was the best) to theme each company weekend away and to send everyone off with something memorable which was related to the single-word message that was core to that year's success. We chose a single word because it was something that everyone in the company understood. The goals we presented on PowerPoint were then printed and stuck around the office, while individual targets were often stuck to the side of desks. Copies were also shared globally, and were up on conference room walls for guests to see. If any individual was drowning in demands they could focus their priorities on these key objectives and get a perspective on what mattered most. I would relentlessly communicate these goals internally – and also externally, with key suppliers, customers and any stakeholders that could help us towards success. I am constantly disappointed at how few companies approach their annual objectives in such a simple way.

Talking to your team

Here are some random communication methods and advice for talking to the people in your business.

■ Regularly, and in different settings where necessary, think about the comfort of any environment for the people concerned. Never be on a physically different level to them.

■ The timing of when you talk to your people should always be thought through in relation to the message you are going to give and the kind of impact you wish to have:

- Deliver bad news on Fridays – late in the day – so people have time to think over weekends, and if necessary (for really big bad news) plan a follow-up meeting for questions the following Monday.

- Always deliver good news on a Monday.

- Always talk to new arrivals on their first day.

- When you have a continual change project to report on, outside the normal reporting for a special project, set a sensible time convenient to everyone involved if at all possible. Establish that this is the time the matter will be updated in order to stay on top and to maintain momentum. And continuity of communication in such hideous situations as a redundancy process can be much more constructive than allowing destructive whispers to germinate. Keep things open as much as possible, and set a standard that communication matters and that it is always two way.

- Announcements like staff departing need to be planned correctly and celebrated appropriately with thanks. Who knows when a person may come back to you?

- Following communication with an open door/private approach policy is important. Irrespective of the outspoken nature of some of my team, knowing my door was always open was priceless to some of them.

- If there are 'missing persons' during important meetings, get a note writer and have messages emailed. And during all company updates make sure a confirmatory email summarising key announcements follows, for everyone to read and take in.

- Engagement is difficult to engender in a company, and sometimes you need to set standards and always encourage a cross-view of opinions. Consider the questions you might expect if there is a sensitive issue at hand and plan your response – though in practice I rarely did this as I felt an honest response to questions was always the best way. I used to hold impromptu meetings, the sort where I would simply enter one side of the office area and ask people to stop what they were doing and come to the other side and have a casual 'wanted to let you know' (and ask any questions) session. Every meeting people came with pen and paper, and I would often also make something up to encourage participation of some kind in everything we did.

The impromptu meetings that I used to call as we grew were frighteningly powerful. I would ask a random group of individuals to give me feedback on any range of topics. They might include products, some of my battier marketing ideas, any bugbears I might be having, and often brainstorms for a particular presentation or offer that we were putting together. Sometimes I gathered a group of suspects in the office simply because I was lonely while putting together a big scary offer and I wanted to show the team what I was progressing. I suppose I was showing off to some extent, but I was always looking to improve – and many brains are better than one.

- Communicate regularly, always be as upbeat as possible. When there is bad news, give it straight and then talk about improvements to leave things positive. Also get others in your team to learn the 'walking round the room' kind of individual conversations that need to happen to keep a pulse on your company. You cannot be aloof, and you must always be cheery and say 'good morning' whenever you arrive at your offices. People watch the way you communicate all the time and you will be setting the mood of your company in everything you do. I was by no means perfect at this but I have seen many who were worse, and the damage to their own success – and mostly the respect in which they were held – is huge.

Sharing a culture

My approach to work has always been that all players work hard for each other. We were a very small unit, and our open-plan office helped enormously with this approach of role sharing. It is crucial that no one is an island in their role in a small company; you cannot have a closed approach and gain maximum momentum. It seemed to me that I should work the hardest as this was my plan we were living, and in leading by example through hard work I found others gave me far more of their time than I deserved. The early team at Pacific Direct worked extremely hard, were flexible to an unbelievable degree in all sorts of areas and set the foundation for the level of care we engendered throughout our global organisation as the business grew. Indeed, they worked additionally hard to maintain and cherish all that positive energy, the celebration, the laughter and expectation of value added through continued learning.

Work was basically fun. We shared the roles, we shared sample packaging, we shared different skills and backgrounds, we looked out for each other. From the outset office politics was decidedly not part of our game plan. Pacific Direct set out to stretch and develop all the team members from all the parts of the company – suppliers included. The enjoyment gained out of seeing others achieve things they never dreamed of is one of my proudest memories from running Pacific. One thing I never did was ask anybody to do anything I was not willing to do myself.

Irrespective of this, we also always made it clear that we wanted more than the best from individuals – but any time they needed extra support, Pacific's policy was that family came first. How can someone work to the best of their ability if things are not working at home? Flexibility is vital. You should always employ great people and they are undoubtedly worth being flexible for – you will always get back much more than you give.

In the old days, when there were only a few of us, if I went on holiday and a decision had to be made, the others went out of their way not to disturb me while I was away. There was an understanding that they were trusted to make a decision; that it did not matter whether they were right or wrong but that they simply progressed, though obviously with the intention of success. When I returned I was often told, when necessary, the thinking that had been put into the decisions made in my absence. They would ask themselves what I would do, and that was the beginning and end of the conversation. It took thirty seconds because they knew me so well. If the decision felt uncomfortable but they also felt it was one I would have made, they knew it was probably the right thing to do. They would also raise any concerns about culture, and it is people like these you need to hire for your organisation. Once you have them, find ways to cherish them.

Develop a positive culture

I had an exceptionally open culture at Pacific Direct. You too can develop and create to your benefit the same dedication, loyalty and long-term staff retention that all adds value to a company. Here are some guidelines.

■ Mistakes are truly OK. Encourage mistake-making openly, and support the action of others when making decisions. We even had a sum of money with which any member of staff could put client service mistakes right, and do so through any means deemed to be a solution. No justification was required – just an implicit understanding that if it was business progressive (client proactive or customer care) then it was fine.

■ No witch hunts after an event. Of course you should learn from mistakes, though. Sometimes you make bad decisions, but it's not the end of the world – and that applies to the people who work with you as well.

■ Do not expect even your most loyal member of staff to be as dedicated as you are and do not get frustrated by it. People do need to be continually encouraged, but it is not their business and they do not live, breathe and suffer in the effort of continual improvement in the same way you do. It is your company – you should work smarter, harder, sometimes longer and you should continue to sweat the small stuff and make tea and coffee for all from time to time.

- You don't always need the latest, greatest piece of technology – but in our business a new member of staff always got the latest technology to show we had invested in them.

- Show some emotion. I have even been known to cry my heart out when trying to describe and recount the long-term loyalty of people who had stayed in the company at their five- and ten-year celebrations. I have never heard anything so stupid as someone once telling me that crying is weak; it's human, and people need to see your human side. Expose your own weaknesses and your staff will see you for who you really are.

Life was, of course, not always perfect. Despite giving and sharing, training and educating, things will go wrong. How you learn to deal with disheartening behaviour or setbacks may well be the difference between success and failure for your company.

We had, at great expense, developed a piece of software under Microsoft Access, which allowed us to fully record all of our sales activities by customer. This priceless record allowed efficient maximisation of the sales effort. It was valuable record-keeping for the marketplace information we owned and it had developed over the years into a powerhouse of detail on hotels which were potential customers. I found it very uncomfortable when information was stolen from the company in the shape of the database, and the situation ended up in me dismissing (with legal advice) a member of the telesales staff who was abusing her access to our sales information. It was a useful lesson, however, and one for all of us: how safe is your data?

The hideousness of taking a previous member of staff to court was terrible, not only for me but also for other members of the Pacific team. I could have settled out of court at possibly less cost and distraction, but sometimes that is not the message that you wish to transmit. Apart from anything else, it was a point of principle which gave an example for others, and I was never abused in this way again – not least because I added better security into our system of records. This is, of course, a classic example of learning from a mistake.

Getting the right people

While I am on the subject of the importance of building a culture, sharing some of my less conventional interview techniques might be useful (you will find additional staff resources at www.companyshortcuts.com/documents). Recruitment decisions will make or break a company, so get them right. I did what felt was right in this area and with a sixth sense, and possibly again thanks to my own lack of experience, I did not follow a traditional process in an interview.

Firstly, the entry point test. Before we had the luxury of a receptionist, I went out of my way to surprise an individual in reception by being the person to answer the door – I usually interviewed at the back end of the day. By seeing how someone reacted to a stranger, and particularly by seeing whether I could put someone at ease before our chat began, I could gauge a great deal about their ability to cope with differing situations.

The handshake matters, big time. A firm grasp, not over strong, confident, for a reasonable period of time, without hanging on (and certainly not a wet lettuce): those are my suggestions. It is also important that someone looks you in the eye as they shake your hand; there are bucketloads of individuals who look anywhere but in your eyes. This is part of making a good impression from the outset.

Interviewing is about an exchange of information in order to get to know someone. You need to plan the skills you wish to know about – what behaviours or characteristics will be important and a good fit with your company culture. You cannot simply follow a standard format for interview questions and expect to find the right people unless your template is customised to the role and type of person you are looking for – which is possible. I would also say that for some roles a template system is entirely sensible as a way of scoring to ensure each individual receives a fair and even approach. In terms of numbers, I would never now interview more than a very short list of people. Strong recruitment is the foundation of a good business and we came to use a specialist, but in the early days, when we did all this stuff in house, we spent too much time interviewing too many people, and shortening the list by applying a simple 'marks out of ten' note on CVs worked really well for us.

To give some idea of how our shortlist could work, I would perhaps score energetic sporting individuals who were making sales applications more highly than those who were interested in less energetic pursuits: energy levels were important in sales and that was one way of assessing them. I also looked for people who customised their application for a particular role rather than adopting a blanket approach to sending out their CV. Modernity of layout and the opening phrase about ambition would also be important, but for me consistent loyalty in previous roles was a great indicator of someone's character or ability to get on with others. Incidentally, I think the old handwritten letter revealed a great deal about an individual.

Think carefully about the place you interview people in. This can affect the impression someone gives you – and the impression you give them. In the early years, I once got feedback that someone who had done a good interview had not taken the role as she did not like our offices, and I remember thinking at the time that it had been a lucky escape. We needed people who could see through the low-cost, somewhat haphazard Victorian office facility we had at the time. If someone was that particular about the environment, then they would find the duck-and-dive, money-focused, lack-of-glamour set-up we had too much to deal with. We were not skin deep.

Every time I've gone against my gut feeling I've made employment mistakes, and every time I've taken a calculated risk based on instinct I've been proved right. So even if it feels scary or seems risky, if your gut is telling you to go for it, do it. If you don't, you're likely to live to regret it. And who has time for regrets?

I recruited one of my sales staff for the Dubai office in a highly unlikely way – a great example of going with your guts rather than with what one might call a formal policy on recruitment. I was travelling economy on an Emirates flight to Dubai and when my computer ran out of battery power I asked the business class staff to plug it into the power source in their galley. After about an hour I went to retrieve my laptop and get back to work. I was standing in the galley when a man came through. He was quite drunk, gave me his cup and asked me to hold it while he went to the toilet. When he returned, he realised I was not the hostess he thought he was handing his drink to but another passenger, and looked somewhat surprised. We started to chat – his drunken state allowing him to drivel through a nonsensical chat-up conversation – and I discovered he was a Dubai rep in the same trade. (In fact he was terrified of flying and had to get drunk to get on board any plane.) I explained that I was looking for a sales person in Dubai and he mentioned that he knew someone who might be interested. We exchanged cards.

When the plane arrived I travelled straight down to Hong Kong and when I returned to Dubai I set up a meeting with my acquaintance to discover more about the market. I will never forget his shock at meeting the woman he had tried to pull on the flight out – but through our accidental encounter I was introduced to the man who eventually became Pacific Direct's Middle Eastern General Manager.

Lara's laws

- Recruit well – employ the best you can and you will go further, faster and can expect greater returns.
- Trust your team.
- Go with your gut instincts.
- Take calculated risks in recruitment but when you are wrong make swift decisions to remove new people who will not be team players. You may outgrow individuals as your company develops; some will simply not step up – but there are responsible and intelligent ways to manage staff transitions into and out of roles to the benefit of all parties. Honesty favours the brave.
- Keep things open – time and effort and an open communications policy will save you valuable time and money.
- Focus on what you personally do well (which is not always the same as the things you actually like doing) and employ others for the stuff they are good at. You will inevitably be doing too much, be too busy at times. At these points always ask yourself whether someone else could be learning from the challenges you need to let go.

- Never expect other people to do things you are unwilling to do yourself.
- Grab opportunities and have a continuous improvement culture. Do not forget to educate yourself – your skills and abilities will need to change and/or be refreshed as the business grows.

3
Sell, sell and sell some more

Chapter goals

- Prioritising sales activities – building momentum for the rest of your work, which gets done outside sales hours.
- Be unique in whatever self-marketing you do (you don't have to outsource simple ideas to get the market talking about you).
- Sales skills are vital, and it is much more powerful to know how to sell your product. At no point should you delegate selling entirely, nor the learning you will gain from customer exposure. Never entirely relinquish customer contact.

People are important, but without sales a business has nothing. It is not a chicken and egg situation; it is a fact. Unless you have a purchase order from a customer, no other business service is required. I do not buy into the eternal delay factors proffered by business start-up procrastinators who want to establish their entire business platform before selling anything. You have to, in my opinion, be certain that your product will sell before spending any unnecessary funds on any further establishment; you might save yourself a fortune in cost and failure, and you have nothing to lose by working accordingly. You can always get a product delivered, but only once it has been sold.

I know my Pacific Direct business might initially seem like a simple buy and sell product, with a need for some warehousing in between, but there was much more to it than that. We were involved in designing, tooling, manufacturing all components, making labels – and, of course, in creating a whole raft of products using textiles, paper, plastic and porcelain. We supplied artwork skills, project management, marketing support products – but, even given all this, I honestly believe that companies who start with a quality ability to sell, having researched the market, have a much higher likelihood of success than those who do not. I would go as far as to say that those people who cannot sell but who want to run a company need to have the right person representing their product or service from the outset.

In the early days we built a solid business platform at Pacific Direct and, through hard work, tenacity and enormous amounts of persistence, developed a fast-growing and impressive customer base. We most definitely punched above our weight when selling to Forte Hotels – then in the process of changing their name to Granada. It did not occur to me, as we tried to break into the major national hotel chains, why we ought not to 'have a go'. I simply thought that business like this – bigger business – was the kind of business we could serve and the kind of company that would be most likely to look for the best price.

The first product I sold to Forte was a shoe mitt. It was nothing special: white, mitten shaped, used to polish footwear (and mostly provided to stop guests using the white towels for the same purpose). It was not even delivered direct to the properties but sent into their distribution centre. But from there came orders for shower caps and then much greater opportunities and wins. From little acorns...

Although I was somewhat overwhelmed by the scale and professionalism of the competition, I suspect my admiration of their product ranges, their snazzy brochures and their show stands made me all the more determined to compete. Sales success comes with persistence, infectious passion and product knowledge. I remember boasting of our customer retention rate, which was exceptionally high in the early days – indeed, I remember pinning some of my success momentum around this figure alone. Never forget the value of client retention. It is far cheaper to retain the customers you win, than it is to win new ones and risk losing older, faithful, money-earning clients in the process.

High-growth success cannot be achieved without a really well-thought-out offer. Whatever you sell, sell it with passion – with the genuine belief that what you offer is going to make improvements, give customer benefits and deliver a solution of whatever kind to meet the needs of the client. The highest-valued business has usually built a niche offer or a unique proposition, but even the same idea sold better than the rest can be successful.

Many, many activities make up a successful paid-for sale, and the process can be long or short but in my experience it covers a number of key stages – a step process that I was taught by Bell Canada during my time in Bahrain when I was selling advertising space for Yellow Pages. I cannot stress enough the importance of understanding the sales process, or the importance of understanding your product and service enough to overcome all and every objection that you will undoubtedly encounter. Overall, my advice would be not to sell something you cannot be utterly sure you can deliver. Businesses are not built on over-promising and under-delivering; they are built on promises delivered time and time again, with the opportunity to exceed expectations to the benefit of the client – who you wish to come back.

Start to sell

There are a few key things to keep in mind before you begin selling.

In order to be a successful sales person you must put yourself in the proper frame of mind, so wake up every morning with your main objective for every day being to sell. A sales person's first priority is to sell, and getting yourself physically in front of the customer is the only way to do this – so make it happen!

Please also remember that practice makes progress, and you will have to overcome rejection and hurdles. Indeed, on average, seven hurdles will be put up before you win any order. If you cannot tolerate a little rejection on the way and cannot muster the bravery to ask for the sale, at least several times, then stick to admin.

Some characteristics of a successful and effective sales person are:
- being self-motivated,
- positive,
- determined,
- always eager to keep learning,
- persistent,
- honest,
- taking pride in the company and in their work, and
- being organised.

Considering I had literally no sales training when I first began selling, it is amazing how much time and effort I have since put into the education of myself and others leading the sales message. At Pacific we spent a great deal of time perfecting the process, the timetable and the expectations of going through the sales training for each new sales person. The time we, as an organisation, invested in making sure sales people started with great levels of knowledge and the right information meant they hit the ground running. Remember that failing to prepare is preparing to fail…

The seven steps of the sale
1. Cold calling

Cold calling isn't easy for anybody, but the more you do it, the better you get at it. It is important to always keep challenging your comfort levels – this will make you a more effective person. Any sales person should always be on the lookout for new prospects, and I used to stress to Pacific Direct's sales people that they should constantly target one new prospect every day.

Before you begin cold calling, it is imperative that you have all the background information on the business and the person you are going to contact. Be prepared – do all of the necessary market research about the particular company, find out what products they are currently carrying, etc. You must be tremendously knowledgeable and confident that you are offering solutions to their needs. By doing the proper market research you are able to understand the marketplace and establish what the client needs and wants. And before you can cold call someone, you first need to establish who the decision-makers actually are and make sure you are calling the right person, otherwise you will be wasting your time. Make sure you know how to pronounce your contact's full name, too – taking the time to do this might not seem important at first, but people respond much better to someone who is pronouncing their name correctly. (I know the importance of this all too well: I am Lara, not Laura!)

During the cold call you want to be able to build a presence quickly over the phone. Make sure you are organised – have a pen and paper at hand before you begin. Don't keep the call going for very long unless the contact wishes to drag it out, and before you even begin, always ask your contact if the timing is convenient or if there is a time when it is more appropriate for you to call them back. You must prove to your contact that you respect their time.

The purpose of the cold call is to set up a meeting time and not always to sell over the phone. The objective is to sell yourself and the company so effectively that you have piqued the contact's interest so much that they now want to meet you. And finally, do remember to smile while you are talking on the phone with someone – it may sound crazy, but you can tell if someone is smiling while they are talking to you by the tone of their voice.

By the way, one of the best and most powerful ways of generating sales leads, which should be worked in any business, is the word of mouth recommendation from an existing customer. Incentivise these, grab onto them and treat these warm leads with the utmost respect.

2. Introduction

As always in sales, put yourself in the customer's shoes. Once you have set a meeting time you must make sure you show up fully prepared. The purpose of the first meeting is to sell yourself and the company; you are proving to your contact that you are knowledgeable about what you do, and that you can offer solutions to their needs that will save them time and money while enhancing their own customer's perceived value of the business.

Always show up to the meeting armed with brochures (if relevant) and short – very short, preferably – PowerPoint presentations; people remember 70 per cent of what they see and only 9 per cent of what they hear, so pictures are very important. Before you begin the meeting you will initially be greeted by the receptionist or secretary. Make friends with these people as they are the gatekeepers for the decision-makers and can make or break you depending on how you treat them. Incidentally, don't ever be rude, negative or nasty to anybody, and that includes when you are talking about the competition. The more you treat people with respect, and the more positive you are, reflects your level of professionalism – and it will be noticed. Equally important to remember is that dwelling on disaster does not move you on or get you closer to success. Mistakes simply close avenues and nothing is the end of the world – or not in my experience, and I have worked relentlessly to turn every negative into a positive. Do so and your days will be much brighter: full of potential for improvement.

Make sure that you greet everyone by a firm handshake – I've already stressed the importance of a handshake and nothing is worse than receiving a weak one. Also, make sure you look everybody in the eyes – this shows your sincerity and confidence – and always thank everyone for their time.

When you arrive at the contact's office or boardroom, always make sure you sit down last (to show respect) unless they invite you to sit, and if you are faced with a choice of chairs

– as in a boardroom – ask where you should sit. Once you are in the room make utterly sure you have planned the presentation or discussion which you aim to deliver (easier said than done, but without even a five-minute plan you will not be able to work the opportunity for everything you could get). During the first meeting make sure you spend most of your time listening to your contact. This is the only way you can really find out what their needs are.

Make your sales pitch memorably short, competent and factual. State your objectives of the meeting to the contact at the beginning so that you are both on the same wavelength. Ask lots of questions. Conversely, if the contact asks you a question that you don't know the answer to, do not lie. Simply tell them the truth and say you will get back to them with the answer (but make sure you follow up – if you don't, then how are you going to expect the contact to have faith in you further down the line?). Similarly, never make a promise you can't keep. Be honest with people and they will respect it. At some point during your conversation make sure these words leave your mouth: 'Is there anything I can do to make your life easier?' This demonstrates to the contact that you have their best interests at heart and are not simply selling a product or service. And take notes and action plans during the meeting.

When the meeting is over try to arrange another one some time in the future (it is much easier to do this when you are sitting in front of the person than by phone or email a few days later). Avoid odd, uncomfortable departures; make your farewell sentence intelligent. Later on that day, email the contact your notes from the meeting in a detailed manner so that you can clarify if anything was misunderstood.

Do you score your own performance after a meeting? Are you self-critical about what you achieve? Make scoring yourself a habit and learn from every encounter. I have also learnt a lot since I learnt to ask others with me at meetings for their feedback.

One important note here: even at the end of the first meeting, try to ask for the sale. This can be done in various ways, for example: 'If I can meet your quality and service needs and meet your budget, will you order from us?'

3. Recommendation

Once all the details have been discussed, you can recommend a product or service based on what they have said at the same time, so there are no surprises. Discuss key terms and conditions. This usually takes place during the second meeting. You may encounter some contacts who want to go through all the steps in the first meeting – it's not very likely but it does happen – and this is why you should always bring some samples along in case the contact wants to see any products right away (if doing so is relevant to your business). You will also need to quote them a price. This might not all happen during one meeting – in fact, you may meet with a customer many, many times before you get to this point. Try and read your contact's body signals. You can very quickly tell if they are interested or not interested. If they don't seem interested, then ask why – and ask what you can do to make them more convinced.

4. Negotiation

Once a product or service has been decided upon, a price can be established and/or negotiated. The negotiation phase can also be quite lengthy but the main areas to keep in mind are:

- Rarely sell anything that does not make a profit.
- Never compromise your integrity, the integrity of whatever you are selling, or the integrity of your company.
- Never negotiate payment terms unless you are utterly certain that your cash flow can afford it.

One useful trick to negotiation is this: if the customer is trying to get you to lower your price and you really can't go any lower, remain silent for as long as possible. This forces them to speak again and usually makes them realise that this is the lowest the price can go.

5. Asking for the order

Always ask for the sale. This can be done at any point but once a product and price has been set, always ask for the order – but expect hurdles for you to overcome. As already mentioned, this can be done casually in the first meeting. Also, always make sure that you allude to asking for the order in any correspondence with the contact: 'I look forward to hearing from you soon and taking your order.'

6. Contract and/or agreement

All relevant paperwork is to be signed and the order is placed. A forecasting schedule can be included where necessary. It is very important that whatever you promise you can do for the customer, you make sure that people within your company are aware of it. You need to keep all of the internal players in the loop in order to have everything run smoothly, and you cannot just expect other employees to adjust to meet your demands.

Here is another method that should be priceless to business organisations that compete in a tender system. Find out as soon as you can the methodology and the value that your buyers put on the different sections of any bid you make. Focus on the big, highly valued deliverables and make sure you meet all the measures placed on the tender. You can find more information at www.companyshortcuts.com/documents.

7. Invoice and/or payment – and the rest

The account now needs to be monitored and maintained. Remember that no order is complete until the money is in the bank. This is sales' responsibility and sales people should not be paid commissions on an order until the business has recouped their costs and been paid, at which point profit should then be proportioned.

The service you provide for the customer doesn't stop once the payment has been made, either. It is all very well to close a sales deal, but maintaining the level of service stated in the contract is crucial; customer retention is just as important. And once the original sale is closed, you have the perfect opportunity to begin up-selling the customer more things – for instance, items for the coming year, reordering products, etc.

If I have one skill which has been priceless in pursuit of success it has been my ability to sell. Right now, I cannot think of an entrepreneur I have met who could not sell their product. I believe I can sell anything, and I believe anyone can learn to sell and also enhance their skills continually by continuing to learn. New skills need to be practised, the most powerful of which for me – keeping quiet, and thus actively listening – has been my biggest challenge. Here, to emphasise how important they are, are a few basic tips:

- Never be embarrassed to take notes.
- Summarise actions at the end of a meeting (use the same document internally and externally).
- Act according to the promise you have made, and fast – the sooner you deliver on the promise, the sooner you make money. Take the early appointments every time.
- Follow-up efficiency wins orders; always think about the next sale development and building long-term relationships.
- And don't be 'British'. Over and over again, people who are persistent, leave more messages, make more calls and ask more often for the sales, make more money.

Phone skills

Is your answering machine message on your phone everything it can be? Do you always leave a call-back number? Do you always sound confident, bright and cheery despite having the worst of days when you answer the phone? Incidentally, how often do your team hear you selling by phone? In an open-plan office you can learn from each other. I cannot stress enough the importance of an open base of all communication and how much value this gives.

When calling customers, never, ever ignore an opportunity to leave a solid message. Indeed, when calling any customer take the time to leave an energising, original and entertaining one. You need not appear to be unprofessional but the originality of a message that amuses will always have a greater chance of getting a positive response.

There is, of course, the eternal debate over phone messaging services on direct lines and the means of communicating with ease. The point in everything is to give the client what they want. We concluded that our luxury five-star customers wanted to speak to someone intelligent and able who cared and who, in one touch, could pass them on to somebody who could answer their questions. We had the world's best receptionist, but we also bothered to train everybody in the business about call handling and the different kind of enquiries and the people to whom these queries should be forwarded. There is nothing more annoying than wasting time finding out, through three different calls, that the person with the answer you need has left the building. Do not do this to your customer – aim to make every single touch point with the client smooth, efficient and professional. Your client handling is a representation of your brand, your image and the service you sell. We all form opinions on the service we experience and, directly linked to this, we all make conclusions about the company in general. Your employees represent your brand and your product, so work hard to ensure they do so to the best of their ability – from day one. Think about your customers. For instance, I could not employ people with an accent that could not be universally understood as we were an international business. At one stage we even taught all our staff how to transfer a call in French; we had French-speaking housekeepers calling in from all sorts of time zones and we needed to guide them to the right people to maximise success.

One last important sales tip, call wise. Set yourself targets for outbound selling goals. When it is one of those horrible days when it seems you are not having much success, just keep going – often the next best client is only one call further away from the last rejection. I used to call over 150 people a day, or perhaps more in the early days. I did it with the old-fashioned use of a roller-directory card system I created myself using library leads, and I would play games with myself, starting back, front, middle, different letters or whatever, just to keep the game interesting and original (I even used to score myself points to mark my success rate). I rigorously applied successful previous sales-call conversation pieces, which engaged the client until I completely perfected my phone pitch. How hard have you gauged client reaction to what initially will be uncomfortable and difficult for you? Have you then prioritised which are the most valuable conversations, always starting with the highest? The more calls you make and the sooner you make them, the sooner your success rate will grow.

Image

Let me touch on your own personal image. Conformity has not been something I have found comfortable in life, and there is an inbuilt mechanism, I think, in many entrepreneurs that looks to beat the odds. Being memorable can mean something simple like being dressed appropriately (which still takes thought and planning) all the way through to being dressed inappropriately with intent; creativity with a touch of originality can overcome barriers. But do remember this: if you are confident enough to be outstanding, you had better be good enough to deliver on any promise you make. I have often and still do wear odd socks deliberately, but at the heart of anything, we will always be 'measured' by first impressions – so whenever you have the chance of promoting your business, dress for impressing.

Irrespective of the entrepreneurial tendency to be nonconformist, I would suggest that nearly all successful people have respected a dress code and know the time and the place in which they do have to confirm to one, to a presentation of themselves which will allow them to make progress. The way you speak, dress, stand, eat, drink and every detail of your person is under scrutiny when you are selling – and many of us are selling something every day. Certainly when you are building a brand, you are the leader of the brand and everything you can do to represent yourself in the appropriate way matters.

I was selling to luxury five-star hoteliers who know better than anyone the importance of dress and presentation. I have undoubtedly met some of the most beautifully turned-out and elegant people in the hospitality industry, and I have learnt from them the efforts to which they go to present themselves and their hotels to the best of their abilities. If you are, like I was, wanting to be taken seriously, then present yourself in the right way and style yourself to suit your industry; even consider the pen you write with and the watch you might wear. I have learnt to dress down for some appointments and dress up for others. Think hard about respecting the people you are meeting, consider the impression you need to make and dress for success. Do not forget to walk tall, and do so with confidence.

Developing the sales process formally

It may sound unbelievable, but we survived years at Pacific without any formal sales literature. Clearly we were very lucky to have managed to have achieved as much as we did through miniature sampling alone. If you know your market and know what the client wants, have great people on the ground and deliver accordingly you can achieve a great deal without much formality.

I appreciate this was much easier given the type of products we promoted – but how lucky again that we checked out what the competition 'did' for sales sampling, analysed it and bettered them in every way… except for brochures, that is. Many members of Pacific Direct's staff called our competitors, claiming that they were about to open a bed and breakfast guesthouse and so were in need of toiletries. We measured the time it took for samples to arrive, how they were packaged, what samples were sent, how they were presented and, of course and where possible, did direct offer-price comparisons. I cannot stress strongly enough the importance of competitor research, and it will come up again, but in the meantime realise that if you are not already monitoring the sales process of your competition, you should be doing so. You will learn a great deal which you will be able to use in the improvement of your own company.

In the early days we were fortunate that we never had any clients visit Pacific Direct, only suppliers. The advantage of this was that the clients had no idea just how low-cost and small a company we really were – and the suppliers who visited thought we ran a 'cut to the bone' operation (I suspect they went away knowing we were mean and lean and truly needed the best price, too). I believe these early days of cost savings and retention of profit through overhead control stood us in good stead and underpinned the culture we had. We wasted nothing, not even scrap from misprints, which were turned into message pads.

Incidentally, in 1995, I did manage one world-class achievement outside Pacific Direct – I married Charlie. He returned to the UK from Hong Kong to live with me and even work with me. A high-risk plan but something we decided we could make work, and we did. One of the few pieces of work we did together was finding a data programmer for a software programme that we had custom designed for managing our sales contact base, which was growing well beyond our old-fashioned card management system.

The new programme recorded the key data and activities for the customer contact as well as all standard core details (and I'm afraid it still makes me giggle that our excellent IT advisor was called Phil Daft). Anyone, at any time, could refer to the customer in detail and know where we stood, but most importantly I could divide the sales force into different groups, and sales team members literally managed and churned through these contacts and reminder activities on a daily basis. It was outstandingly basic and all we needed as a method of sales management, and I am certain the scale of control we gained through the adoption of this database enabled huge value creation through capturing leads and opportunities.

The matter of data management and ownership is – or should be – a great concern for all business owners and, as I mentioned earlier, we learnt this to our cost. Some will say with resignation that they expect sales staff to steal sales data (what a shame, but probably realistic given the ease of thieving and transporting information contacts). New systems like salesforce.com – a system on the internet, which Pacific moved to in latter years – are more secure platforms with better restriction controls. Whatever non-sales people would like to think, getting sales people, who are notoriously bad box-fillers, to complete information systems for the benefit of anyone but themselves borders on madness in terms of likelihood. I count myself as a salesperson and if there is one thing we all loathe doing – unless it has a direct material gain which is easily understood – it is following systems and processes. This will remain the continual challenge of every company owner. You should recognise the ongoing battle to get people to conform is worth whatever data capture you make, as this is a valuable source of asset in any growing business.

Customers first – service ethics and attitudes

You must have a customer-first service ethic and attitude in every part of your company; after all, the customers pay your salary and retention builds a business. Your cultural values must put the customer at the centre of all the decisions you make in development and investment into your business. Staying in touch and being at the coalface is critical. This is much easier in the early days, when you will perhaps have time every day for face-to-face client meetings, but it becomes necessary effort later on as your business outgrows your direct individual sales drive.

I do not remember formally learning anything about customer service; all I have ever thought is that in order to be able to be the best, the company I represented needed to deliver consistently on its promise. In those days we had phenomenal client retention rates which supported our huge growth rates – and by the way, a lost customer can be the most powerful learning experience. If you ask your departing client why they are going elsewhere for a service you have previously provided, you may discover a great deal about the shortcomings of your operation against the better offer from a competitor. In my experience you will be surprised at the level of detail a customer will be willing to provide which will help you improve for the future.

One of our more entrepreneurial and adventurous ways of introducing our business to our customers in a different and memorable way – and at low cost – was when I joined the Housekeepers' Association in London and the Midlands. I attended as many events as I could and built relationships which remained in place during the development years and onwards throughout the success of the company. Are you a member of your local trade organisation?

The opportunity arose for Pacific Direct to sponsor an event for them and I came up with a scheme to educate our customers in how soap was made. I paid for coaches to collect housekeepers from London and drive them to Buckingham one afternoon to visit our soap supplier, the newly established Buckingham Soaps. Winter months meant timing was tight as we needed the housekeepers to get round the small plant quickly in daylight hours, and we hired a baked potato van to feed them during their visit. This wasn't exactly five-star catering standard, but despite being run on a shoestring budget the event was a huge success. It was something different for the Association, something educational and interesting – and it was a captured audience for Pacific.

Five-star customer services performance standards strategy

Here is a list of the activities we relentlessly practised at Pacific Direct to ensure the best levels of customer service at all times. Use it as a model.

■ All our team members were recruited in the full knowledge that they were expected to be continually committed to improving overall customer satisfaction – indeed, to continually improve anything that made the business better.

■ A three-ring telephone policy. This policy became the benchmark for our customer service expectations. Simply put, if an incoming phone call was not answered within three rings we could gauge how we were behaving in the light of aiming to achieve a customer-first policy from the outset. (Achieving it was sometimes a nightmare with team players in meetings, during holiday periods and at other busy times, but this is when the culture really began to build and the simplicity of the message permeated all that we did.) We had to literally preach this objective and had ambassadors to manage expectations. When I phoned into the office I would always congratulate excellence in the way the phone was answered; I rarely had to comment on a poor, unattentive, unenthusiastic answer, as there was simply no place for that in our standards.

■ All queries and messages were responded to within four to six hours (including emails).

■ The majority of customer complaints were to be satisfactorily closed with client confirmation within twenty-four hours; otherwise further time was mutually agreed.

■ Telephone/fax acknowledgment of purchase orders that were placed.

■ A delivery questionnaire was despatched at least twice a year to 50 per cent of the top 125 client base

■ We measured overall customer feedback and satisfaction through a methodology we called RATER: reliability, assurance, tangibles, empathy and responsiveness – with particular focus on the last two.

■ Clear objectives and Key Performance Indicator measurements for staff ensured highest standards of professionalism and service – and don't forget to reward the behaviour you need people to exhibit.

■ Two 'career development reviews' for each member of staff a year.

The relevance of this to customer service was that if team members were not happy, we could not expect them to go the extra mile with customers.

■ A dedicated sales manager supported by an account manager was assigned to each customer account, with holiday cover pre-planned and announced in advance.

■ Sales consultants visited key clients regularly to discuss mutual objectives, goals and opportunities. You must make sure a visit expense is covered in client profit value, and set the levels at which a client is valuable enough for a face-to-face meeting.

■ Adopt a consultative approach – 'We won't sell you unsuitable products, we will sell you original and innovative products.' At Pacific Direct we said that 'we intend to advise and guide in the decision-making process and to offer leading edge brand product solutions at best fit for client demands'.

I would also suggest that you make very sure what your business capabilities and boundaries are. What does your business not cover in service? Are your team clear about not wasting time discussing something that makes you no money? Having said that, there is no harm in helping a customer with an introduction or source for a product you do not do – this is sales point scoring and is in the area of building client relationships; it can be a great foundation for a new and developing relationship. I often encouraged our team to give references for other companies in our field and beyond. Often I recommended a solid business which distributed the disposable products our hotels bought, and to some of my clients the introduction of such a great service only served to emphasise the value of the offer we made.

Do not undervalue the importance of hearing, first hand and not through sales feedback or through marketing, but direct from the client, their evaluation of your service, your product and anything else which effects their buying decision. Invariably customers have great insights into product development throughout your competitor base. So learn to listen hard and look for eye-widening excitement when a customer asks if you can deliver something new, something which may well have been introduced as an innovation by your competition.

The measurement of customer service standards also depends on your supplier base. We used to bonus-motivate our distribution company for performance. We had a contract which promised that they had to deliver goods within three days, but we promised clients a week – so they were almost never let down. We relentlessly demanded the best possible standards from our subcontractor, and never blamed them for a lack of service performance because I saw these choices of extended service as still being our responsibility. If a supplier that you have selected lets down your customer it is your fault and you need to take ownership and resolve the problem. (You may also have to look at the issue of the supplier not meeting agreed and established criteria, of course.)

Incidentally, the only time when the customer is not king is when he or she behaves in a way that is simply unacceptable. In our case this was manifested in the way one individual spoke and behaved when ordering from our team. This particular customer always ordered late, outside standard policy and always pushed time boundaries, and in the end I took some delight in calling an important hotel in London and informing their Purchasing Manager that we would not be doing any further business with them. I made the call from the middle of our office, in the sight and sound of the core sales and service team. I cannot underline enough the value of such a lesson in putting your own team above others in a situation like this. The reinforcement of my utter faith in them was extremely powerful.

Lara's laws

- Your sales passion is infectious and must lead in company development.
- Stay in touch with the customer, always.
- Aim higher than you initially plan, you will be surprised at how your audacity delivers beyond expectations.
- Process speed in the sales cycle is vital and makes money. The faster you narrow down objections, the sooner you win the order or move on – and both are progress. Keep pushing.
- Complacency kills, persistence pays.
- Be entertainingly professional and exude energy; it breaks down barriers.

4
Getting sorted for growth

Chapter goals

■ Create opportunities through new markets; even international expansion is not rocket science.

■ Doing the right thing by your people matters, communicate in all sorts of ways – and keep demanding ideas for improvement.

Looking back now at the haphazard nature of our international development at Pacific Direct, I cannot reasonably call our approach a strategy. Because of my upbringing I saw the world as a small place, and fortunately I had developed a product range which was suitable for selling on a global platform. It could well have been disastrous, and I do wonder how many companies reach such a tipping point. I have proved that with great people, considerable trust and undoubtedly luck (though luck made through hard work), much can be achieved. My naivety and lack of business training enabled me to buck a system I knew nothing about. Today – with experience comes restricting knowledge – I would find it much harder to make the same impetuous moves without greater concern for potential failure. Is there something to be said about the blind faith in success that I held then? There are undoubtedly a lot of advantages in being young enough not to know better.

In the early days of Pacific creating a memorable reputation was not difficult given my natural character and the advantage of my relatively young age. I also have my mother's boundless energy, but I believe everyone can train themselves to have more energy – eat the right food, stay fit and practise. It is not about the number of hours you work but how you apply yourself during those hours. Nevertheless, the person with the ability to focus for longer while 'working smart' will achieve more. As often said, business is a race – a quick professional response to an enquiry, the samples which arrive first, the best possible follow-up, the continued persistence to win business: all these count towards growth.

Effort in equals reward out. I was lucky in starting my business without the wisdom of experience. Twenty-three is young, but it's by no means too young, and now that I have the horrid restraints of experience I would recommend this to anyone; the disarming advantages of youth far outweigh the restraints of age and responsibility. Having made appointments by phone with anyone and everyone of significance who had buying-decision-making power, directors would often be very surprised at how young I was when I turned up in person. On reflection, I also now recognise that making appointments can be easier for women – so if you are female, count that as a positive fact in business, one to be used intelligently. Use your voice on the phone to your advantage; I have learnt ways to use my voice, like all great sales people, to get what I need according to my situation. I can be ridiculously emotional and expressive but the power of persuasion by telephone –

and most often by putting a positive outlook on things – gets you a long way. If you are well-prepared, speak knowledgeably and with confidence on the telephone (sometimes adding the right accent), then anything is possible. And it was one of the factors which enabled our international growth.

Irrespective of hindsight, I am not embarrassed to recount my past business international development decisions. Why? For two reasons. The international growth we embarked on, with sales endeavour always leading the supporting office expense, works. And because other people, I hope, will learn that sitting back is only an option if you wish to be beaten.

I see and hear of too many people waiting for help, spending time looking for assistance, delaying with research into international markets and hoping that someone is going to give them the golden nugget of success. You will make your success by creating opportunities. To create opportunities you have to discover, through passion and daring, the potential in new markets. There are limitless global opportunities for growth that are untapped by businesses who spend too much time waiting and not enough time pioneering. Now, more than ever, it is the small, fleet of foot, flexible business models that will be first to markets whilst the big boys flounder. The privilege of being self-employed gives you an often-forgotten power of choice and the freedom to do what makes sense. You must trial and sometimes you will fail, so learn from these mistakes. I did not think I threw caution to the wind. I simply used my knowledge, listened to the customers and weighed the odds of my success. Growing a business is not an easy affair; if it was, there would be many more leaders and fewer people following your potential success.

So to the ridiculous nature of Pacific's international business growth strategy, such as it was. There are companies who bellyache about the lack of international government support (there can always be more) and there are those that see the inexpensive price of a trip to potential new markets as exciting opportunity, an investment worth making. I would encourage – indeed, plead with – any business leader to go and discover by travelling to new markets and working it out for themselves.

You will be amazed what you can achieve in a short visit to a potential new territory (ideally linked to a show of some kind on your industry sector, because you can learn loads at such events in the shortest of times, get to know the competition and save a great deal of time, rather than looking on from afar). With travel costs so inexpensive this kind of time investment should be irresistible to most leaders.

You can spend your time worrying about government regulations and rules, and use excuses not to develop your company. Yes, of course check out the basics – start with duty import rates into the country you are interested in, perhaps ask the British Embassy or High Commission what they know about product demand in their territory, use the technology at your fingertips to understand the basics. But don't get bogged down; you will find more practical information and help in chapter 6.

Small-sized business growth is the easiest phase for freedom without burdens, which can weigh down bigger businesses, so milk this stage while you can. You are under the radar and as things grow you can comply accordingly. I accept that challenges and red-tape demands have grown, but frankly these hurdles are administration issues; get on with it and get back to selling.

Growth will create challenges...

Pacific Direct opened an office in the USA. Why? Well, at this stage we were considering all sorts of changes to the company – including the creation of a new division – as I believed there had to be a better way to approach smaller hotels and properties through the creation of a mail order brochure which would offer a one stop shop.

Time and time again in my travels I had come across a book known as the buyer's bible in the hospitality industry – the *American Hotel Register*. At around a thousand pages long, this book sells everything a hotel might need, and I mean everything. They had just started a launch in the UK through their US General Manager. I was most impressed with him and asked if he would like to join Pacific Direct to drive my new division idea, but just as we were about to employ him, he had to return home for personal reasons. I liked him so much and believed he could bring huge value to Pacific Direct, that I decided to offer him the chance of establishing our US office. He did this with huge dedication, brilliantly setting the foundations for Pacific in the US. (The hospitality mail order catalogue launch died, incidentally, although today someone else offers this mass-market solution in the UK with great success.)

Around the same time, the Dubai office was also founded with a similar lack of business planning. Nevertheless, having done my own market research, it was quite clear that the potential of the Middle Eastern market was huge. At this time – 1998 – Pacific Direct was not particularly focused on only supplying luxury branded goods, but the client led our strategy and we learnt to focus wholly on their luxury demands. I knew from previous experience that setting up a Dubai office made sense if we were early entrants.

I always knew it was a somewhat 'missed' market and I had the privilege of feeling very at home there due to my previous sales experience in the Gulf. For some time we acted as a trading company and in later years we established a professional and locally sponsored company set-up there, but either way the selling momentum has remained.

Between 1993 and 1998 we all worked incredibly hard. Like all business leaders, I found it exceptionally lonely running Pacific from time to time. I don't think I ever believed that I was really on top of anything and everything, and I have always felt I was fluking my way from one big challenge to the next. I encouraged others, relentlessly, to learn and grow their skills. I read business books and equally relentlessly applied the ideas and concepts that I read about to the company. I worked constantly to motivate the forces of Pacific – time was invested in constantly communicating with the team, constantly including them in developments, constantly supporting team players with visits and talking through the challenges they were experiencing. Sharing our success with everyone was a foundation of the way I felt I needed to manage. Nevertheless, I had at this stage no formal model of how to measure and manage the business, and I was losing control.

I took a lot of decisions based on gut feeling and managed to build a momentum of growth that was considerable for a company of our size. Towards the end of that period, though, the complexity of our offering was becoming overstrained and I knew we were lacking a core strategy. Like many who are growing outside the small-scale single leadership/dictatorship control, I became acutely aware that I needed help. We were overstretching our cash reserves (and, in fact, all the resources of the business). It was at this time that I started looking for help from outside the business to grow my own skills, something that was desperately needed to bring our next phase to its full potential.

In flying by the seat of my very uneducated pants, I always strived to challenge any status quo. My upbringing taught me to be ambitious and to always do my best. Blind ambition is pointless – but focused, determined and planned shared ambition can be enormously powerful. And so I encouraged questioning, review of systems, process or anything that pissed people off. I often had the team gather round and write down answers to three questions I would bring. People could choose whether or not to write their names on the paper, thus allowing brutal demands and honesty in response.

I posed questions such as the following:

- What could we do to improve the office environment?
- What wastes your time every day? (One of my favourites.)
- If there was one part of your role you wish you could cease doing, what would it be?
- Is there anything you think we could save money on by making a change?
- What idea have you come up with recently that you think we could adopt to improve anything?
- Which piece of office technology wastes your time most or causes unnecessary stress in your day?
- What perks do you think we are missing in the company that we might consider for future improvements?
- What projects could you offer others in the business so that they could learn and take on greater responsibility, and also learn from being challenged outside their comfort zones?

You would be amazed at the value of the responses I got.

There are a myriad of questions that are appropriate for different phases. Not enough companies work hard enough to engage their teams, nor work a continual improvement culture. The pointless effort, fruitless report writing and people with value not being encouraged to add value is all wasted profit potential for those company owners who treat their people like mushrooms.

You can endlessly pose questions to which the answers will vary in scale and benefit. You do not have to have the whole team in the room; no one will feel left out in impromptu sessions (as long as they really are impromptu) and you may discover that the purchase of new coffee cups or teaspoons is as valuable to some as the option of changing your freight costs is to others.

People and the pitfalls of growth – a path littered with learning

At the stage of high growth you will be hit with the double whammy of outgrowing some of the skills of the loyal team you have built. At Pacific Direct we had limited – a neat way of saying no – staff structures of any kind at this time, leading to people being under ridiculous amounts of pressure, without clear guidelines and no real measures for performance expectations. Fortunately at real peak service demand times my team continued to perform beyond the call of duty. A wonderful example of this is a terrific customer services lady who voluntarily drove to Birmingham on a Friday night in order to deliver the soap which a hotel needed for the weekend, having first driven to Luton to collect it.

Sooner or later you will have to find the time to manage role splitting and sometimes create new positions to allow for the recruitment of new players with higher skills. This recruitment time will also further drain your resources, as will the induction and training required when new team members come on board. The fun time will soon become a thing of the past unless you plan and delegate to ensure that you stay working on the business – and allow, encourage and train others to step up with you. Of all the skills needed during this time, one of the most important will be the ability to help take those employees you have developed thus far and lead them to greater potential. There is little more rewarding than seeing individuals challenge themselves to take on greater leadership responsibilities, and enjoying their success. You need to create a path of potential and share that direction with your team.

Employing and engaging individuals at work must be a core focus for any leader who wants to create a bigger company. Staff retention, development and motivation should be high on the list of priorities for management – a dedication to getting the best out of those you employ will always pay dividends but, better than that, employing those who have the right skills for the role is a critical starting place.

Remuneration can be a minefield. As with many small business owners, your team will grow around you with no structure of employment rules or grades of terms, but sooner or later as the business grows formality must be introduced for fairness and the benefit of all. As a company grows so do the range of roles, skill sets, even hours of the day and places you require people to work – combined with where they work, what they bring to the business, and what the market will pay for the same role. (In the early days I didn't really have a pay scale, and to some extent that remained the case, as I felt that in general each individual is worth whatever you are happy to pay them for the value they add.) It is always worth getting the local recruitment reports on what core roles are valued at in your area; it is also worth always keeping a recruitment specialist on side and keeping one eye on how market trends affect the employment opportunities for the individuals you have and want to retain.

It has been proven time and time again that non-cash incentives matter and rate highly in a person's choice to stay in a role. But more significant than anything is the impact the person they report to – their direct manager – has on their enjoyment of their role and their willingness to work. Performance measures and career development reviews (appraisals) are necessary but, held in the right way with a constructive genuine focus on the individual, these opportunities are priceless in terms of moving the company forward through the improved skills of individual employees. The cost of replacing experienced individuals is huge, perhaps two or three times their annual (not monthly, note) salary. That makes any incentives you offer that produce results cheap compared to the pain of staff change. Pacific can be rightly proud of the long-term dedication of the team from the early days, and I have enormous pride myself in the fact that we were successful at retaining staff – but you do have to work at this.

Training and development must not be feared as they are an opportunity to grow individuals who might otherwise leave and go elsewhere. People who have learning opportunities and who feel they have a development path will stay and continue to add greater value. The belief that 'if my people grow, they might go' is simply idiotic. Would you rather have mediocre staff without skills? That, frankly, is a no-brainer. I worked my people and openly celebrated those who continually went the extra mile, and in return they stayed, giving the business stability and the long-term, priceless knowledge necessary for growth.

Do not underestimate the value of peer-group learning, either. For example, we used to share skills in the office to bring each individual up to a more than basic level of Excel and it never cost an extra penny. We had a resident genius, someone who enjoyed doing macro-creative tasks at weekends, and I am sure that type of person exists in most companies – someone who will relish the chance to share their passion. What can members of your team bring to others? When your team attend a course or skills development session, do they bring back ideas to share and benefit the rest of the business?

As they grow, too many companies mismanage the responsibility they have in the whole process of staff recruitment and employment responsibility as a whole. People are not numbers and should be treated as individuals. Nevertheless, individuals should also have responsibility for their behaviour in the company, and providing clear understanding of expectations from the outset is important. (When I used to do the recruiting, I would say to potential employees that at Pacific we got more than our pound of flesh, but it was given willingly, and that the days would rattle by.) You can find useful checklists on www. companyshortcuts.com/documents.

Another key point as you grow and recruit is the importance of selectivity. Recruit slow and fire fast. And when you reject people who apply for roles in your company do so with respect. Sometimes people have all the skills in the world but you simply do not feel they would fit the culture of your business at the time. How you say 'sorry' has the potential to either bring great negativity or build your reputation. We worked hard to hit the right note at Pacific, so please take a look at one of our rejection letters. I think it makes a positive out of a negative:

May I thank you for your interest shown in Pacific Direct and for taking the time to attend your recent interview, it was great to meet you. On this occasion we are unable to offer you the role.

At Pacific Direct we recognise how daunting it can be to attend an interview with great hopes of becoming one of the team, then to find that one is not accepted. It is in no way a reflection of your capabilities.

However, I would like to take this opportunity to encourage you to not be disheartened, we actually have a member of staff here that was successful at interview at the fourth attempt. She has now been with us for five years and is a valued member of the team. I wanted to share this to demonstrate that determination and strength of mind, along with the right opportunities, will undoubtedly lead to every success.

Please accept my congratulations for your excellent interview and I wish you every success in the future.

Once people were recruited a little sense check was introduced as I became more distant. I was often travelling when new team members joined, so I would ask people by telephone how they felt their induction was going. This was sometimes followed with an email in which I would ask the new recruits to give some statements about the company a score:

Out of a possible score of ten, where ten is best and one is worst, what is:

- Your experience of the PD team in UK, support wise.
- The training experience, now that in essence it is complete.
- The reputation of the company in the market as you have experienced it.
- The quality of marketing material.
- The quality of the team overall.
- The quality of customer service approach.
- The quality of the way we share performance information in comparison to others.
- The technical support.
- The communication in general.
- The office atmosphere and surroundings.
- The terms of contract you are under.
- The system of recruitment in relation to:

- An original process and interviews.
- Have we delivered on our promise of the kind of company you expected to join?

Sometimes it was amusing to hear the shocked reaction of someone on getting a call from the CEO who was thousands of miles away. I am not sure I let anyone else know about these little 'sense checks' at the time, but I felt the direct feedback I gained from key additions to the company was always useful. As the company grew the importance of me bothering to touch base with new recruits in this small way became all the more powerful. Make the most of the value new starters can bring to your business. Encourage fresh ideas, suggestions for improvement and also encourage them to settle in. The faster they are up and running, happy and comfortable, and the quicker they are valued, the sooner you will be repaid.

People really are the core of your success, so treat them as such. One of the most successful people-development tips I learnt and tried during this time came from yet another one of the business books I had read in transit, though initially I thought it manipulative and icky. I spent nearly five hours on a flight handwriting individual cards to each employee, cards that were specific congratulations for great performance and outstanding contribution. I carefully wrote a message of encouragement for achieving more in a particular area of weakness, and ended each one on a positive note of thanks. Despite my initial reaction to the author's suggestion the time seemed right, and I put all these individually selected cards in each person's in-tray on the same day. I remember as if it was yesterday the resounding responses to my private, carefully constructed missives. Some people cried, some laughed, some quietly reflected, some chatted to me like never before and some wrote similarly constructive and encouraging notes back. The power of the pen does indeed remain much mightier than that of a sodding email.

Learning for growth

Despite all the growth and excitement (or perhaps because of it) by 1998 I was running a company about to turn over £4.5 million, with no qualifications past those in scuba diving and a few A levels, and I was no longer enjoying what I was doing. For the first time since the start of the roller-coaster ride I was drowning and unhappy, and I remember describing to one of my then 'on call' (unpaid) mentors that I felt overwhelmed. For the first time I was feeling negative stress. I kept being dragged into small daily issues where team members had not stepped up to new responsibilities, mainly because I had not trained them or communicated new boundaries of accountability. I was running a company with a wonderful cobbled-together Excel solution to most things but limited automation (nil integration) and high growth. I concluded that I needed greater business education – at almost any price.

At this time I never really stopped to think about how much fun I had been having and how much I enjoyed working with the group I was lucky enough to have attracted. I still did not really understand the scale of what we had achieved until I finally felt forced to step back and really review my company – guided by business professionals and peers.

In those days the best way to learn was to go to one of the best business schools in Britain. In 1998, with the business growing fast, I decided to go to Cranfield Management School to get a business education, and this was the first time I had really invested a significant amount in my own personal development. Everything I'd done until then I had done on instinct and common sense. I knew I wanted to expand the company; I also knew I would need to learn new skills in order to do so. The amount of information available to entrepreneurs today from all kinds of sources is really staggering – and all of it is useless unless applied.

I researched the Business Growth and Development Programme (BGP) at Cranfield and applied to attend with the following year's intake. I did not realise at the time that my little company would be researched for its credibility and fit on the course – and, once I did, I took an entirely new approach to the power of company information available from Companies House onwards. (Incidentally, you should regularly purchase a copy of the accounts of your top suppliers and competitors – not to mention getting annual general meeting reports from publicly listed corporates. These hold priceless information, from business performance and profitability to important and powerful names of directors, as well as being a wonderful resource for your negotiating power.)

Cranfield might have been a little taken aback by my first few weeks on the course, but rather impressively – and somewhat memorably – they took my approach in their stride. There were forty-seven male participants on the course and three women, including myself, and then there was the addition of my newly born and still breastfeeding second daughter (by this time I had perfected a technique where, balanced correctly, a baby could breastfeed while I used both hands to type). I had warned Colin Barrow at Cranfield of my challenge in course attendance, but I knew that with the help of my husband and our world-class nanny I would manage to attend the whole course. Let this be an example to other entrepreneurial women; you really can have it all (sleep is overrated, and over the years I learnt how incredibly well the human mind can perform even when sleep-deprived).

While I was at Cranfield on the BGP I learnt an immense amount – how to write a funding request, how to properly use recruitment services, how to better understand the talents of my team. Not only was there value in education, but often lectures underlined the natural skills and ability that I was already using at Pacific. During any lectures I found dull I would put time in towards planning ahead, and time spent in the bar was priceless as I finally had time to talk to other business owners, people who all shared similar concerns and dilemmas. (I was surprised how little the other course members knew about distribution costs and process, and the importance of competitive knowledge – both of which are priceless.) The power of the course in confirming that I was going in the right direction was a massively beneficial take-away for my own self-confidence. Indeed, without Cranfield I would never have known I was running what was then Britain's fifty-seventh fastest growing business – a Dunn & Bradstreet independent report had been published in a business magazine I would otherwise never have known about.

I also managed to really stand 'above' the company for the first time, working on but not in the daily business chores, and I left the course with a very clear plan for my future objectives. I cannot underline enough the power of attending a course which ensures you review, or even write a business plan and have it tested by other independent but constructive advisors. Of course – like many training offers – you have to decide what works for you. It really opened my eyes that other leaders from different companies could gain outstanding benefits from a lecture in which I could see no new value.

One of the major decisions that was affected by my time at Cranfield was the further improvement of our IT systems. We needed a completely integrated software program for improved efficiency gains, as we were well past the stage of being able to grow on our complex Excel-based systems. Most businesses cobble together processes that work in relation to client demands over early years, and knowing when to invest in real IT systems is one of the most paramount decisions a business leader will make.

We needed to make our enterprise more efficient. To do this, implementation would be focused around standardisation of tasks and how we could simplify any business process activity. This review would lead to possibilities for automation and, in the process, the more we could simplify what we did, the more time we would have for selling. More time for selling meant more profit. Herein lies a challenge, though. Standardisation is the first step towards achieving greater efficiency but some companies have their ability to remain flexible and agile in the process of winning and retaining business beaten out of them. Whatever system we invested in had to be grasped and passionately applied from the top down or else it was doomed to fail.

This is a major step up for many organisations. It's a big part of the change from being a smaller company to becoming a professionally integrated and efficient bunch of people who all have to follow process steps to deliver the right end result. In the meantime the system also has to reduce duplication, time-wasting mistakes and finally provide a much more valuable set of reports to allow the further development of the company.

One more valuable asset of the Cranfield course had been the knowledge I had taken from one of the other entrepreneurs that there were university departments looking for projects, some with funding to help small businesses develop systems and processes (I am not sure about this availability today). We approached Coventry University, presented our need for support and found them to be nothing short of excellent in the help they gave in defining and finding the right software program for Pacific to invest in. At the start we had no really clear idea of the kind of money we would be talking about

– of course, this can be a massive figure, but the cost of our fully integrated platform investment was around £100,000. Given the results it allowed and the cost savings we gained in process improvements and efficiency gains, and the fact that the system would set us up for significant extra growth, it was a necessary investment for the new foundations of our next phase of growth. The technology platform I invested in cost nearly the same as my first year's turnover. Had I not reinvested retained profit into the company, we would not have had the accelerated growth in place to afford such solid foundations. Too many owners mismanage reinvestment priorities, and at this point their finances become overstrained.

At roughly the same time I was making significant changes to our strategic intentions for the company. My Cranfield learning, combined with my knowledge about the global market and the interest our major competitors had shown, plus what I had learnt from them, gave me clarity about where our sales focus should be. Mostly driven by the wish to be niche and my desire to maximise our company value through a unique proposition, I made the decision to drop all our invested stock lines at 56 per cent of current turnover that we were then carrying. At the time, I felt strongly that this was the best strategy that we could have; I gave little thought to the possibility that my clear new direction would fail. Luckily my approach paid off.

At least I recognised that the scale of the major players was something near impossible to compete with, and that the way to avoid their threat was to sell to a part of the market they were little focused on and which I felt quite knowledgeable about. By 1999, due to our overwhelming customer-service success in the UK, we were really selling all things to all people without any focus. Until I went to Cranfield I did not really do the analysis of profit that I needed to do in order to really grasp where we made great money. I was gradually coming to this realisation before Cranfield, but the work I did during my review of the Pacific business performance gave me utter clarity on the way forward. I decided to focus entirely on the luxury end of the market.

As a small business owner, if your faith in yourself and your own instinct isn't strong enough, you won't succeed because you won't take the next step. This is something my team understands as well. It's about moving out of your comfort zone, stretching yourself, testing your abilities, growing your knowledge, experiencing something new, and then trusting what you 'feel'. But in order to do this you have to know your business inside out.

Lara's laws

- Create a culture that expects continual improvement and constantly communicate that this is a team effort in which every person adds value.
- Any business grows in step phases but profit retention and maximising efficiencies must be the heartbeat of success. Your commitment will allow investment possibilities to set solid foundations, making the big decisions easier to action.
- Your people must want to grow and learn to keep up their own skills, adding further value the longer they stay in your company. Retention investment through really working at caring for the team gives immeasurable potential for improving growth.
- Never stop learning new business skills or challenging your own competency – expose these abilities and you will gain much from other people going through the same turmoils.

5
Hallelujah, it's misery day – finances first and always

Chapter goals

- Understand the importance of equity ownership.
- Share skills around, staying on top of the right stuff that you should be considering and continually reviewing it.
- How you can grow without external financial investment – use the banks.

All business owners must think very seriously about equity, and do so right at the start. Today I endlessly hear company owners considering the sale of equity as a method of growth.

Indeed, often I find that companies have been established with a split of equity being poorly thought through, with a lack of real appreciation for what the value of each individual share could stand for in the future. Pacific Direct started with a hundred shares that were worth nothing. It sold for £20,000,000 – with each share worth £200,000. Please think through very carefully, at the set-up stage, exactly who has what in equity shareholding. Please, and at all costs, do everything to find alternative financial means – at nearly any price – rather than surrender equity for cash.

Equity is your most valuable asset, and equity dealers cannot build businesses which is why they trade equity. It is your sweat, tears and worry that create equity value – so relinquish it slowly. You may have to starve a little to hang on tight to high levels of equity, but it will be worth it.

Cash is key

Although I was by no means perfect, my understanding of the importance of money and my paranoia on knowing the numbers served me exceptionally well. On any given day I could have – off of the top of my head – given anyone an accurate immediate overview of the debtors, creditors and cash in hand. I am lucky in the sense that I remember numbers well, but I worked at that ability. I've always liked the impressed reaction when I can remember to the penny the important and not so important figures (including any unpaid children's pocket money).

When I first started Pacific Direct – and right up until the point where I sold it – I would always carry round with me a checklist of questions which I would relentlessly ask myself about the performance of our business. It became my bible. Often I would have a copy I could scribble on, highlighting some points and simply ignoring others that were not requiring focus at that particular time. The key to its effectiveness was regularly reviewing it and checking it for sense, as well as constantly improving on the reporting quality, analysis and application of the information as I studied our success.

You will catch busy-fool disease if you grow without focus. Busy fools do not make the same big returns as those with a solid grasp of the boring numbers. I would sometimes ignore all other demands on my time, even when drowning in my workload, to review our performance and ensure that whatever activities I was intending to do did indeed add value.

What drives value?

My checklist looked like this:

Maintained profit growth through a combination of:
- Sales
- Cost control
- Business efficiencies

Guaranteed order book
- i.e. Contracted sales % of top 125 Key Performance Indicators
- Contracted business importance

Product quality and longevity
- Brands
- Contracts
- Continuity of reducing reliance on leader and improvement in overall sales dedication

Competition placement and competitive edge analysis
against competitors
- Continual comparison/review, relentless need for
  continual improvement to stay ahead of the game

Solid operational / supply chain

Clarity and completeness of all business functions
- Accounts / HR / Sales / Purchasing / IT etc.

Physical assets – appealing to needs, assessment of
added value (office refurb?)

Location and market penetration

Current main quarter must have focus

Employees skilled and knowledgeable *but also* shared skills

Image
- Marketing the culture of 'customer first' attitude from
  every part of the business
- 'Better and different' ideas and continual improvement
  from all
- Unusual parts of promotional activity, focused on what
  works for ROI

Data
- Peaks and troughs
- Sales and production
- Margin analysis 80/20, trends – year end
- Stock analysis 80/20
- Competitor analysis
- Strengths and weaknesses, focusing always on what
  we do well and resourcing accordingly

Business plan
- Sales trends
- Production capacity – planned in advance value added $
- People/recruitment needs

Integrity, confidentiality, reputation – rigorous family attitude, with big-company, commercial professionalism feedback/approval challenge

IP/partnerships – pride licensed references/what other awards to strive for to add value/reputation and create publicity?

Cohesive management team

One vision and mission

Healthy cash flow

Website modernity and momentum

Balancing all of the activities on such a checklist is nearly impossible. Imagine you are polishing the steps on an escalator. My view on business is that the minute you have polished the step that you are about to step off at the end of the ride up, it disappears. At the base of the escalator, just as you step off, the same step appears again. Previously bright and shining, it has got dull while it ducked out of your focus – and this is the ongoing puzzle and challenge of alignment. However, keep running on the escalator and you will have a really good chance of making things work. (On a literal level, I am still the one to the side of any Tube escalator walking up the steps, always wanting to be the first to the top.)

Incidentally, there's a powerful mathematical hint for ensuring that you are always adding value to your business. Calculate your own hourly rate – and work out what you will potentially generate for the company if what you are working on delivers. If the resulting calculation does not give you three times return on your investment of your own time – considering you will also be a drag on other resources – then don't do it.

Irrespective of any knowledge about all the component parts that make up business success, the facts are stark. Without cash management you have nothing. Your number one priority should always be knowing where your cash is.

Squeezing the lemon

Here are some tips for cost control, especially in the early stages:

■ Buy your furniture second hand or at auction.

■ Buy your computer equipment and software first hand and invest heavily in computer training – for everyone. (I made the mistake of assuming the senior players we recruited had these sorts of skills and then found they depended on 'administrative support' in order to do the most basic tasks. I often found I needed to employ two people for the price of one.)

■ Buy quality paper only for outgoing formal offers to clients. Limit all stationery investment by rigorous control and have a policy that all message-taking is done on the reverse of redundant printouts. By the way, do not forget the power of a fax, even today – a piece of paper landing on someone's desk is a refreshing change from the endless email traffic, and might put you in a physical in-tray faster than someone can click the delete button.

- Team members can do all sorts of tasks to save funds if bribed openly with pizza or other refreshments. Things like sample packaging/promotional mailings/sending newsletters can all be arranged during lunchtimes, and a lunchtime food rate is a lot cheaper than paying for outsourcing.

- Utilise all free labour including offers of work experience which can be a massive benefit for all – particularly during busy times. Apprenticeships might also be worth consideration, as all parties win for a relatively low wage at the start. However, do not treat work placements as being anything other than an extra team member – individuals will add huge value if they are there to do more than make coffee and tea. One of our temporary staff once came up with a simply brilliant 'language' for us to use in managing the communication of our stock – the traffic light system could not have been a more straightforward approach and saved us time and money.

- Save recruitment fees by word of mouth messages. We had a policy of advertising jobs to the internal team when also recruiting from the outside. This gives every team member the opportunity to consider a role change or progression, or to tell friends they rate and think would fit in. There is no better gauge of a potential employee's character than those people who will have to work with the person who is potentially being employed.

- Stay fit and walk and talk for straightforward meetings. Many of the Pacific team kept trainers at work and walked and talked during lunchtimes. This is not just a way of keeping costs down, but a sanity stride round the park can also do wonders for refreshing the mind.

■ An end-of-day lights off and computers off (and not in sleep mode) policy saves money and sets the right message for all employees to consider the environment.

■ Establish early on a travel and hotel stay policy. Economy flights from the outset was the norm at Pacific and remained the norm until I sold.

■ Postage can cost business a fortune, so set a policy for determining which parcels go by what level of urgency. You will be amazed at what you can save by good mailroom management, and the same applies to sending out brochures, samples and catalogues. This is a good example of an area where people feeling they belong makes a difference. They will look out for the small stuff that really adds up.

■ I have already mentioned my 'three quote' buying system when I discussed getting accounts advice in the very early days of the business. This is a priceless way to check that you are buying the best, so apply it to all your procurement needs – and regularly test the incumbent against others so the main provider keeps their prices sharp.

You can always buy in expertise in the form of subcontractors, and one example is appropriate here (though it's also a general cost-saving point: we did this in other areas, notably finance and recruitment). I made a seriously rewarding investment at a time when we had been stretched but I felt the budget could not afford a full-time role in professional buying. I turned to

Andrew Botting, ex-Granada Forte Buyer, and he helped review our warehousing services, among other things. I only had to pay him by the day and the return on this investment was significant considering the chunky savings he made. This kind of buying review should be an automatic process for business owners growing into the mid-scale.

■ Limits on who had company credit cards definitely saved expenses – especially coming on top of a rigorous expenses procedure that I would check from time to time.

■ Giving time away is a priceless reward if you cannot afford cash. At Pacific Direct, sunshine might mean an early-finish Friday, when we would announce ad hoc early departures for the general team, with management staying behind to man the phones.

■ Short-term leases with easy early break clauses give you plenty of chances to move office.

■ Outsourcing IT network support – something we did throughout my time at Pacific Direct – is money well spent. Incidentally, we also used off-the-shelf packages for all our accounts management and reporting software until we got to the size where we still used off-the-shelf packages but with about 15 per cent of customisation, which was the next best ticket. (In the end we invested heavily in software sourced through our Czech division, saving us the expense of buying at UK prices.)

■ Referral sales make growth easy. Deliver on a service promise, fight to retain all your customers and then get those loyal fans to help introduce you to others.

- Simple premium gifting paid dividends to Pacific Direct we can never calculate –inflatable sponge ducks, 'get it done today' memo pads and large plastic memo clips for housekeepers to arrange their papers were all reminders of our brand and intentions. Small gifts like these can work for almost anyone.

- Never pay sales people commission on a deal until the money is cleared and in the bank. This should be any company's standard practice for long-term security.

And finally, if your business culture includes the belief that everyone is rewarded out of the same profit pot, and all the savings add up and impact that profit potential, you'll be amazed at how much more conscientious people are. Get people to treat the business's money as their own and you have cracked it.

The importance of all of this can be seen by looking at phases in the financial management of Pacific Direct.

Phase 1 – my 'skin in the game'

Pacific Direct was started on a shoestring; it was a bootstrapped business before I knew the meaning of the expression. All I knew was that I had £17,000 in savings to live on. I had learnt from my father to always know where the money was, and from the outset of Pacific I always considered cash impact and demand in any decisions I made.

In 1993, and despite meticulous care and representation with my accountancy firm, I was rejected by Barclay's Bank when I requested a £10,000 overdraft facility. This was also despite an enormous order book with pre-signed new business from some very well-recognised hotels. Banks were reluctant to lend. I was 25 years old, a one-man band, had a limited business track record and was reliant on one major supplier from China, which was very much an unknown entity then. I hate to admit this, but on reflection and knowing what I know now, I suspect the banker who turned me down backed the odds of me being unlikely to survive. My first year's turnover was £108,000. My second year it was £360,000, with a decent profit. My third year's projected sales (most of them booked and on contract) were £800,000 – significant growth.

Rigorous cash management, polite conversations and requests for improved terms with suppliers, and careful collection management had allowed us to grow up to a point. I pumped every penny of profit back into the business. I never abused the company as a lifestyle business and only in 2000 (after nearly ten years) did I buy a company car – and even then it was second hand and from a friend who desperately needed cash.

The other significant and highly valuable tip I should underline here is that finance is not only about cash management, it is also about the knowledge of costs in any company and the impact these costs – and any change to them – have on the company as a whole. I wonder how many companies which fail have been running without accurate product costing systems? By 'system' I mean a spreadsheet that simply lays out, to meticulous levels of detail, product production costs from the point of purchase through the production and sales process. Near the end of my ownership of Pacific it became more challenging but not impossible to know the contribution and/or margin mix of a range of products we were selling across a global platform. But from day one smaller companies have no excuse for not knowing exactly how their profit is made up.

Determining the sales price to the end user when I first started in business was done by taking the cost of the item itself and then applying a calculator multiple to add margin of varying levels of degrees, depending on what the company established as the 'standard' margin. I look back at this fact with horror as the missing detail of all the variables of cost can be so vast that intricate products – with exceptional client requests, particularly those that require customisation – can very, very quickly wipe out all profit, making the time and effort spent expensive and highly risky.

If you do not know and cost in all the parts of the process that enables a product to be made, delivered and invoiced – and within this all the touch points that impact profit – then you will not survive for long. You will not remain competitive, nor can you do deals based on volume and other such client demands. Most importantly, you will spend your time being distracted by areas of the business where the actions you take simply remove you from being wholly focused and in control of the profitable parts of your business, those which really deliver.

In the early days of Pacific I developed a basic spreadsheet, which was revised again and again over the years until we developed the ultimate version. Determining the costing structure of the global costing format was a long way from item by item, broken down, freight-allocated sales costing sheets, but both served the business with an awesome platform for all of the players at Pacific to understand where we made our money. Many businesses, who have never done this properly, do not actually know where they really reap their profit – and the assumptions they make are often quite wrong. At Pacific, things moved on from spread-sheet management with a macro system showing a range of profit of items in a mix of articles sold, and the complexity of our costing methodology should probably have been moved to a computerised system earlier. But the foundation upon which we grew the company relied heavily on sales people being educated on the product pricing side and allowed us to accelerate our growth, while understanding entirely where we could make the most.

The costing sheet Pacific Direct perfected over a number of years became, I think, a part of the reason for our success. Initially only two of us used the costing sheets, as we were the sales team. Over time the use of the costing sheet (and its complexity) became a critical part of the induction training process, and the sheet itself was fine-tuned to include all the details required to allow us to really understand the difference between net and gross profit. All members of the sales team knew how to use the costing sheet, and so did all accounts team members, the sales administrators and, of course, all the management. We also developed the costing sheet system into a document that we could apply to global tenders, which rolled out into cost-management systems for the company-wide pricing of global offerings – products that we had to cost inclusive of delivery and duty to allow us to really gauge cash-flow planning and profit on the deals we wanted to win.

We often had to subsidise the margin on one item over another in order to win a mixed item supply, but allowing the sales people the ability to duck and dive in this way – even though it might seem risky – was very powerful when combined with a commission scheme that paid out on deal profit. A sense-check mechanism for the costing methodology which I had applied was developed and rolled into a cash flow and profit and loss impact statement. This also allowed us to plan bigger financial needs. Currency always remained a risk in our global trading and at the time I sold we were looking at hedging currency protection.

For me the secret was costing control linked to cash reinvestment in continual growth – with no sale of equity.

This is something I would like to advocate to all – though not to the level of control, necessarily, that I took.

Just an aside on the vital importance of margin management and the understanding of how this is directly linked to maximising exit value. Simply put, if you can squeeze the hell out of margins and maintain a market competitive sales price – retaining profit throughout – then when you get to exit, the multiple you may achieve could be considerably more than it would be for those who do not build this thinking and behaviour into all their company activities.

I hardly paid myself any money in the very early days of Pacific Direct, and I would still suggest that this belt and braces approach to maximising your early days' opportunities is the best. Banks want to know that you are not greedy. Once you have served your time and accelerated the business's stability, you can change your income and start to reap some of the rewards. You will also find that when you are asking a bank for money – an overdraft, loan or any kind of credit – this kind of behaviour bodes well in the building of a trusting relationship. The stupidity of not spending time in building a relationship with your bank will hold your business back. You will be paid far more attention and taken far more seriously when you need bank services if they know your history and have an idea of your track record. It is not difficult to send monthly management accounts to a bank; even when times are tough, stay in touch and be frank about your challenges. Banks simply cannot tolerate surprises.

By this stage in Pacific's development I was really learning and living by the saying 'what gets measured gets done'. Hence the vital point that when you set measurements and indicators, goals for people to achieve, you must, must, *must* target the stuff you need done by priority and forget just measuring stuff for measurement's sake. Having said that, setting a time for discussing performance against targets is also a critical feature of the processes you need to set as you grow.

Cash availability is not enough, although you should know your cash available at the shortest notice. You should also have a picture of what this is expected to look like over the following twelve months; banks will expect this at the very least. You need it to know when funding requirements change and you should know it intimately enough to spot trends which allow you to think and plan actions in advance.

Here are the reports we used.

■ Cash burn (weekly/monthly) is the proper measurement allowing you to make sound sales decisions with financial control in place. This attitude will stand you in good stead with any bank and is critical in allowing you to do the most profitable deals – a luxury which some companies who do not grow as fast as Pacific do not have. Profit on the deal, including the time that it pays you back in, is the real cost of the cash applied to a deal and you must make your spending decision on the whole picture of funding a product through the sale and payment. Then, and only then, you can make decisions on what is really the most profitable piece of business you want to take on. When cash was very tight I put a great deal of effort into sales in countries where a letter of credit business growth was possible without a drain on cash, and utilising extended credit facilities from suppliers with whom we had relationships.

But how do you extend supplier relationships without damaging the flow of goods? You bother to call the supplier whose terms you might be stretching, who is also benefiting from your growth, and you talk to them when cash is tight. You then agree a revised short-term payment plan and you stick to it. Too many people ignore the fact that the suppliers' possibilities are affected by your slow payment – and in effect you could be shooting yourself in the foot. Clearly a balance needs to be found when it comes to the buying decisions you make. Try and estimate the impact that a new spend might have on the company. A big spend obviously needs time and research, but ultimately if the system is not working and you are wasting funds, then you need to put in step changes immediately to stop the rot – perhaps applying cost savings, perhaps trialling a new approach – whilst you continue to squeeze the value out of the deal. To a point, though. Never go beyond what a supplier can afford to sell to you for; service will be provided to the level that you are paying and in the end your business may suffer. The big boys sometimes squeeze great deals and make them work as the smaller companies suck up additional expenditure whilst the power of the volume scale works for their buyer; it's annoying, but that's life. I have seen wonderful examples of consortium savings in the hospitality industry – do these exist for your business?

Cash burn should report how much cash you are going through (burning) on average in a week or month. Divide your bank balance by your cash burn and it will tell you how many weeks or months you have until cash runs out. You must always know this figure.

- Debtor days – recording your average collections performance. If your payment terms are thirty days and your debtors days are currently at ninety, it highlights a problem in your collections department. Poorly collected cash leaves money in limbo that you could be using. Whilst our sales growth remained exceptional, we milked every penny as fast as we could through the system and had world-class in-house collections ladies who handled their role with immense pride.

- Creditor days – I hate to admit this point, but the fact is that I measured the time it took to pay our bills, and we set what we thought was a reasonable standard by which our suppliers could plan and know they would be paid.

  Our industry payment terms were thirty days, month end (and are you clear about what yours are?). This means that most major companies in the industry order, if possible, on the first day of the month and pay on the last day of the month following that month – nearly sixty days after placing the order. This cash outflow delay sometimes allowed us to do deals and grow extraordinarily. I am afraid I would advocate slow payment to major suppliers time and time again if it allows you to grow more quickly.

- Average sales per sales person (and, in our case, sales per region per month). You need to establish which members of your sales team are 'rainmakers' and which are not, and you need to have a team of rainmakers to maximise product potential. We could not spot a poorly performing sales person in a few days; indeed, it took a few months to really establish a sales person's performance. Nevertheless, the tracking itself and open shared targets achievement are time and again proven to bring better results from a team as a whole.

- Sales sum (sales summary). Allow me to introduce to you our daily reporting system. This showed the market sales by sales person and a running total, monthly and annually, towards the overall sales goal. The percentages it gave appeared to show competitive gaps between individuals and overall performance towards monthly targets. Everyone at Pacific (and I mean everyone) had access to this every day on their email. I know for a fact that at the end of the month shipping, sales admin and inventory management departments – when working at their optimum – would work closely to ensure that every penny was delivered, shipped and invoiced to achieve and overachieve the goals for which we all shared responsibility.

Our systems reported to us annually at costing (before the sales stage) both the net and gross margin of the goods we intended to sell, by item, by range, by any scale set. Systems like this will save a fortune in unprofitable decisions to sell goods. Nonetheless, something we only cracked towards the end of my ownership was the ability to report sold goods' actual margin against expected.

■ Average gross margin. At the end of every month our accounts department produced a wonderful report showing the reported profit per invoice and highlighting any customers showing less than appropriate profit for an order. These invoices then become the responsibility for the sales people concerned to put in a price increase, explain themselves if this was an exceptional blip, or sell something else that would bring up the overall margin above a company-set measure.

Additionally, I learnt to use ratio reports at Cranfield. These allowed a completely new view on the numbers and were incredibly powerful when considering our performance overall – and when measured against those of the competition.

The early days of a business, when everyone is multitasking, is a great way of seeing how you as a business are performing year on year. Efficiencies can be lost as a company grows, but this measure will ensure you know where you stand as you perhaps invest in new structures and efficiencies to take you to the next stage of growth. I do see this as a stepping-stone system, and sometimes you quite literally are speculating/investing to accumulate in the next phase.

■ Revenue per head/overhead per head. Divide your revenue and your overhead by the number of people in the organisation. Knowing whether you are top heavy (or not bringing in the revenue to support the headcount) will be priceless in making employment and any other important cost decisions. I would genuinely sometimes procrastinate over employment decisions even when I knew the team were hard-pushed if the numbers did not support the role in the long term. Do not waste time in a recruitment process you cannot later afford.

It has been said that 'consistent' self-funded growth (growth from always retained profit) was one of the major performance points, one that – without knowing it at the time – played a big role in the growth and value of Pacific Direct. I do remember being envious of those who attended training courses with somewhat snazzier cars, those who appeared to have far more relaxed lifestyles and those who appeared to be more organised and relaxed that I ever was. I had understood from the outset that cash was king, following my father's bankruptcy, and I also felt I never wanted a complex organisation where I was depending on the company for everything. Pacific Direct was built on a self-funded, profit-generated, working capital basis and never required additional working capital funds outside its normal banking facilities; indeed, we were often cash positive in the latter years.

Phase 2 – the use of factoring (a dark art)

In 1995 factoring was a very new offering from the finance community. Much misunderstood and often quoted as expensive, this form of bank borrowing nevertheless allowed Pacific Direct to continue its fast-paced growth without relinquishing equity. All of the language was new to me but I learnt how to use the factoring system and for me it was the only choice for continued growth.

Given that our growth in sales was immense, we were spinning off excellent profit per head and retaining that profit in the company. The problem was that growth was so fast that we required even faster cash release for us to increase stock holding and service our clients' monthly demand for toiletries.

I cannot remember the exact terms (though I do remember being told by all around me that factoring was very expensive), but I distinctly remember in those days the significant negativity from clients about the fact that the management of my invoices and payments was being given to 'strangers'. I did not see factoring negatively – it was the only way I could grow continually at a pace, by getting up to 90 per cent of our invoice value the day after it was raised – and handing over our collections seemed a perfect fit for Pacific Direct. However, I also listened carefully to what my customers told me and worked hard with the factoring company to ensure that the relationship and client contact rules were utterly clear. Pacific staff were told the importance of the relationship and we worked very hard to ensure that our representatives from the factoring company saw themselves as members of Pacific. Even though we did not actually employ them, we did indirectly pay their salaries. I developed the relationship we had with our collectors as much as I could, and would insist that Pacific team members visit their offices and learn their roles so that together we made the best of the system on offer. Whoever is the collector in your business, love them; communicate with them continually and stay on top of cash collection at all times.

From a financial point of view, by 1999 Pacific Direct was overstretched and the global management of the finances was becoming more and more complex by the day. We had 'bought/established' ownership of two factories, set up an office in Boston USA, and launched our business in Dubai. We were already trading in a number of currencies – the US dollar, Renminbi, Hong Kong dollar, sterling, lira and soon would be adding the euro. By the time I went to Cranfield one of my big needs was to establish much better financial controls. I knew that I was going to have to go to the bank and – if the growth rate continued, which looked likely – ask for a considerable overdraft facility. This was a scary thought.

While I was at Cranfield I sat next to a man who had just launched a management buy-in with funding from 3i. They had imposed certain conditions, and initially he felt that a financial specialist had been 'forced' upon him. Only a few weeks later this man was raving about the specialist, Nigel Alldritt – a fine lesson in never judging a book by its cover. I scribbled a note asking for his contact details.

Nigel came to visit Pacific to have a chat about the chaos I felt we were in, and his arrival will always be remembered as one of my luckiest strikes. He was entirely too qualified to work in our business full-time in the early days, but his brilliance and the input he added on a day a week basis – at a daily rate which then made me wince with pain – gave me personally probably the highest return on investment of any of my employment decisions. Do not underestimate the value of a part-time role such as this, as it might be just what you need in your company.

Perhaps the frankness and open-natured trust I displayed to Nigel encouraged him to help take up my challenge and become our part-time Financial Controller – or perhaps the enormous range of financial management that we required appealed to him. What I do know is that from the moment I met him, he established a group-reporting platform for monthly management accounts like nothing we had had before. It took literally years to develop a standard which provided consistently reliable performance information, but given that Nigel worked with Pacific players in China, Hong Kong, the USA, Dubai, the Czech Republic and the UK, over multiple time zones and multiple skill levels, the role he played in Pacific is legendary. It is also notable that I was able to access the skills I needed without actually employing a full-time specialist.

Pacific had always grasped every development in technology quickly and invested in it (often for free, with the right bank) to allow us to run efficient and transparent accounting practices. I recognised from the outset the importance of credit control and the risk in supplying international locations – where you lose all legal reach once the goods have left your jurisdiction, so your money is at risk – and hence the importance of trading in terms that ensure you do and will get paid.

During the Cranfield course, and with my recognition for greater financial controls, it soon became very clear that an overdraft extension was going to be very important to our next big step. Whilst at Cranfield I attended a brilliant lecture, one which – to this day – I value more highly than any other lecture I have attended. It was presented by an ex-banker and was about some critical details: the information required by a bank for lending considerations. We were taught about the different levels of debt, and the process around which the bank would, in normal circumstances, regard the risk and therefore price the lending cost to a business in expansion. Most interestingly for me, and certainly an important point that I will always refer to, was that I learnt the importance of establishing the different levels of approval required at differing points in the scale of lending.

What I mean is that at the local level you will have a business banker who, depending on experience, will have a certain ceiling to which he or she can lend without senior approval from the branch manager. The next decision-maker is inevitably the branch manager, who I think in my case had an upper lending approval limit of £150,000. Above that figure, the decision was moved out of her hands and put in the regional hands of a lending committee in Birmingham. It was incredibly useful to know this, and to know that though we would not be allowed to present the imperative information that I was taught to gather to the 'committee', the way we presented it was important. We needed to give the salient and valued facts by which one banker would produce a report for the credit committee who make the final decision, and to whom the business owner cannot often speak directly.

You might be, as I was initially, terrified of owing huge amounts of money to a bank. But if you are going to borrow, always borrow more than you think you need and always give conservative figures to show the pay-back timescale, never ones you have any doubt about achieving.

I took the responsibility of my overdraft to the bank very seriously. As a point of honour, I felt that although they were just another supplier (of money), the trust the bank had placed in me had to be repaid with honest and open information sharing and – in the end – full repayment of the overdraft. Living initially with the first lump of overdraft, and sleeping well, came with challenges. But it is amazing how quickly, as you focus on the business and on delivering the plan, and if the results come as promised, you will treat the facility as another asset in your business. One tip: always offer banks a less than ambitious position for growth and always over-deliver, keeping something up your sleeve so that the news can generally be positive. Things go wrong and you need to deliver, as a worst case, the promise you have proposed in your figures. Nothing less than this would be acceptable if a client said they were going to buy a certain number of things from you and they did not, and that is when a bank will also lose faith in your relationship with them.

I am also proud to say that although Pacific Direct had substantial global complexity and dealt in various global currencies, no significant bad debts damaged the business.

Phase 3 – invoice discounting

I cannot remember exactly when we moved from the outsourced collection function back into collection by our own team, though still with the invoice advances paid out. This was the luxurious next step of generating enough profit in the business and being sizable enough to afford the employment of a credit controller. It was also a natural progression for the company, as we became a more complex financial operation.

Complex financial management to me is boring, to say the least. What it was to Pacific and to any other fast-growth business is utterly critical, and not nearly enough companies focus on these absolute basics from the beginning to allow their businesses to flourish. Since selling Pacific I have coined a phrase to describe something I used to do: 'Hallelujah, it's misery day.'

With a clear conscience I used to plan a day a month, usually just past the tenth of the month, where I would spend a day looking at the critical measures in the business that allowed me to be really on top of the company's progress. I would suggest that real value creation is about cash generated, monitored and collected that you carefully and quickly reinvest into the growth of the company to generate greater profit. It is the intelligent – prioritised by profitable return potential – use of the money you make that will accelerate your safe growth. If you do not know what is actually generating your profit, how can you possibly minimise risk and grow at high speed whilst maintaining current earning relationships at the same time? How can you also know which clients you do not want and, more importantly, which you should go to every commercial length to keep?

Financial top tips

1. Be conscious – even paranoid – about cash flow
Fast growth is a common killer of companies. Business owners often celebrate the winning of new orders far too early, without knowing the impact that the purchase of raw or stock product to sell has in advance of profitable delivery. The cash-flow bind created by late stock coming in, slow launch planning and delayed approvals in a development process is always an excuse, but the fact is that a financial controller who is on top of the big-impact decisions must help control sales growth during these exciting times. Doomsayers about trading risks can be the saviours of a company.

Seasonality, new product launches, things like Chinese New Year: all sorts of external factors affect the availability of cash. Finance has to hold a buffer in the event of tougher times and slower sales. You can guarantee that when things are tight something will always go wrong, just to add insult to injury. Knowing where the cash is remains imperative and you must depend on being served this basic information more regularly than is usually required so that you can make quality strategic decisions.

2. Ensure your finance team understands your business and the intentions of the major shareholder

When push comes to shove, the main shareholder ultimately makes the decision on the direction of the company driven by personal expectations. These may be varied – depending on intentions and needs – but, from family-owned companies to privately owned and everything in between, you must have an understood end-goal expectation.

3. Make sure that your finance team helps to drive the business forward

Too many finance functions report colourlessly on standard sets of accounting documentation, without any significant or useful highlighting of trend patterns and changes in the business which could be significant for decision-making and planning. Nigel Alldritt was exceptional at helping me appreciate the core performance figures and he continually added value by using his skills to gain better banking terms, better costs from distribution and improved efficiencies in managing our money, and in minimising currency loss through unnecessary exchange losses.

One of the monthly reports I liked the most was one that presented actual versus budget, simply laid out and perfectly highlighted for odd variances. This was accompanied by a conversation to talk through the month-on-month trend against target and overall performance against the previous year. Pacific was growing fast enough and profitably enough to make most of these meetings enjoyable.

4. Scenario consideration of big growth impact

When any of our sales people were bidding for a considerable piece of business in the later five years of our growth, Nigel would construct a specific deal-related spreadsheet analysis of the cash-flow impact likely from the launch of the new contract, with all the nightmares of stock build and launch delays considered. Of course, such crystal ball gazing is only an estimate, but there are usually precedents in most industries to give trend guides. These analyses allowed us to be relatively accurate with our forecast expectations and allowed me to fix pricing according to likely product performance. The power of being able to demonstrate the profitability of a mixed group of product sales against actual costs kept us secure when bidding aggressively or inventively for major global contracts. A financial department must be included in any deals affecting growth potential – I would suggest those of perhaps 6 per cent or more of turnover.

Although our basic costing programmes were not traditionally run within the accounting function (as is the way in big corporates), I kept the basic costing of products within the sales group. This was in order to enable flexibility and intelligence around sales bids driven by the sales team within certain permissible margin-controlled barriers to entry. I suspect this methodology, with clear control features, enabled fast growth at high margin as sales were paid on profit, never on turnover vanity. Irrespective of this, finance kept a keen eye on the margin performance of each of the product ranges, a measure that was important in setting expectations for bigger-deal evaluation.

5. Outgrowing your bank
You will outgrow your relationship with your local bank, and you must always be well ahead of the game when you know you need support funding for future growth potential. Always ask for cash reserves at the time when you need it least. Those who are too distant, uncommunicative and who do not keep their funders aware of performance –

monthly – deserve all they do not get. You will also buy better (borrow at lower rates) when the funding is prepared in advance of difficult times.

One point about your relationship with funders as a whole is to always have a back-up plan, again in advance of needing it. As with every other supplier, shop around to get the best bargain. Never settle for the first offer or for any single bank proposition; they should be made to work hard for your business just like every other supplier!

You simply cannot make empowered and appropriate intelligent investment decisions without the facts – however small or large the numbers are. Please, please whatever you do, learn how finances work in a business. And if it is not your forte, and even if it is, get the professionals to run your finances so that you can focus on growth and strategy.

Extraordinary things happen

You can never tell where you might find support. This story is somewhat odd, but rather like the oddity of buying a company in Czech (just to continue my supply chain in tubes for Jarvis Hotels in 1997), like many events in networking and general business opportunities you never know where your next big break might come from – or indeed how long positive momentum can last in adding value.

Following the Pacific Direct celebration trip to Barbados, we gained full coverage of our trip on page 3 of the *Daily Mail*. I have framed the article, titled, 'Thanks a million'. All I did was deliver on the promise I made that as soon as the company made one million pounds in profit, in a twelve month period, we would all share an expenses paid trip to Barbados.

The publicity we gained from this adventure was not actively intended to gain public exposure or free advertising but I would suggest the return on investment generated from the knock-on effects of positive value this exposure gave me was priceless. I learnt valuable new lessons as I was astounded by the power of the media publicity machine, where local news feeds into national coverage, which in turn builds reputation, credibility and, where possible, creates new customer growth and profit. (It has been suggested that the profit we were making should not have been shared openly with the public but I can honestly say that the positive response to a company celebrating successful growth, and the excellent cultural benefits far outweigh the negative viewpoint. In any case if you really want to find out how a company is performing it is cheap and easy to trace the company accounts.)

Our publicity caught the eye of a broad mix of people – I know for a fact many employees of other less reward orientated companies, 'celebrated' our press with their bosses. I understand some managed to influence their own inventive rewards targets which no doubt paid dividends to the company owners every time. Even now, nearly ten years on, our incentive scheme is often communicated to me, or recounted to me with a follow up story of how an individual was struck by what many say was the generosity of the reward.

Be very clear, I set a reasonable and achievable open-ended target and ultimately I was the person who gained the most. That more bosses do not share out rewards based on the profits that their companies make continues to surprise to me. We set a new benchmark in original targeting and rewards and we followed up with ideas like the part-share of an apartment, which the company would buy and every member of staff might be able to use for a week. We also thought that a target where individuals each choose a trip of a lifetime would work. I made another mistake in not establishing a new goal soon enough to motivate us through the tough times after 11 September 2001. Indeed it is a regret that I don't think we bettered the Barbados experience until several years later.

The press we gained came out of a chance discussion in networking which escalated into radio interviews, TV exposure and all sorts of add-on benefits for the company. We did indeed set another goal which meant that in January 2008 we paid for the whole of the Czech team to stay in Hurghada, the UK team to travel to Sharm El Sheikh and the Chinese team so spend several days at Hainan Island.

Phase 4 – once again, never forget that cash is king

Irrespective of the cash planning of Pacific Direct and its ongoing world-class capabilities and potential, there is often a time when the risk of investing nearly every penny in a growing concern becomes a burden of some scale.

We were continually risking all the years of blood, sweat, stress and tears that we had injected into the business and this strain – and the growing responsibilities I had to bring up children – started to weigh heavily on me in the following years. The possibility that I could still lose it all, run out of the luck I had continually achieved through hard work, and the fact that I was getting fed up with making family sacrifices was the real turning point for wanting to turn Pacific Direct the asset into cash.

Lara's laws:

■ Boring as finance is, understand it, refer to it and use it as your guide for making solid growth decisions. One day a month is all it takes.

■ Focus yourself on a top few goals – per day, per week, per month and so on – revise them, prioritise them, and always act with the highest profitable return on time invested borne in mind.

■ Take anything for free, negotiate all costs and drive a culture where the team treats the business expenditure as their own. Build this accountability and you will maintain a lean approach.

■ Cost everything meticulously.

■ Count the pennies but afford the best people.

■ Work on your funding relationships and do anything to avoid the sale of equity – *anything*.

6
Exporting made simple

Chapter goals:

- Could your product be more highly valued abroad? International expansion is not over-complicated: visit, discover, learn and make progress.
- Study new markets yourself and don't rely on other people – you can make the decision through a few simple checks on the ground as to whether a market is right for your product.
- Mistakes will happen in exporting. Always learn from them but don't be delayed by the past; business is a race and when all skills are equal, the first one to the finish wins.
- Have no time for complacency.

I am constantly amazed at why small companies do not export more and make more of an effort to sell goods abroad for good margins – with the added benefit of gaining new experiences and potentially wider opportunities. Do not be afraid of expansion into foreign lands. The British, and some other nations, have the enormous benefit of using the English language, and it remains for me a remarkable and unique advantage that not enough companies use to its full potential.

Given my international background, it is not surprising that I developed an initial, so-called Global Expansion Plan. But it was driven out of pure vanity. I used to have to travel to Hong Kong and China in order to work with factories and suppliers from whom I was importing goods. I did have every opportunity to fly direct to Hong Kong, but early on I found that Emirates offered better deals if I changed planes in Dubai. For no additional expense I could have dates that allowed me to stay over for the few days I needed for rest and relaxation on the way home. I used to set myself targets for growth and success (including trip intentions) and in return I would aim to 'treat' myself. Everything was still measured on return on investment but I found that a one-day extended weekend in Dubai – and the tan I gathered there – gave me a huge boost in personal confidence (I bet customers buy more from people with a tan).

I was so focused on the development and drive of Pacific Direct that in the early days my trips abroad always involved weekends so as not to waste selling time in the UK, and I would try and use bank holidays if I could in order to extend my maximum selling opportunities. The Middle East is open for business over European weekends so I could make appointments and sell. I had the advantage of knowing a little about Dubai from my previous experiences. I was also relatively fearless; I was a long way from home and if I made a complete fool of myself, who was ever going to know?

One of the most powerful things we did to establish ourselves in this new and fast-growing market was having the British Consulate sponsor an event for us, hosting all the housekeepers of the hotels in the area. I was very young, probably only 27 at the time, but the enthusiasm of youth and the desperation for success are a driver. It was with great fear that I presented the products and proposition of my company to a massive group of complete strangers. You are only going to be judged by the impression you make, so take my advice: act big and take on the world, the only thing stopping you… is you.

I have often been asked what makes an entrepreneur and, although there are many schools of thought, there are a number of strains in the behaviour of entrepreneurial leaders that sit comfortably with me. Bearing in mind that I did not even recognise myself as an entrepreneur until I took myself off to Cranfield, I can say that I was already doggedly tenacious, persistently determined and always able to find a new direction. I never looked back at mistakes as anything other than a lesson learnt, one not to be repeated, and another positive step towards success. I would like to think that, combined with an innate willingness to work with people towards established and shared goals, these qualities are a fail-safe mechanism for making a business work, but they are not. There are people who treat their teams very badly and make bucketloads of money; there are those who value their teams and, despite some success, have never made big bucks. I think all entrepreneurs recognise that as their business grows they choose to balance on a knife-edge between success and failure from time to time. Sometimes disaster happens, wages cannot be paid and the great guys fail – it could simply be the wrong time, the wrong place, a bad relationship – but the next time they will be all the wiser and all the luckier, as long as they can work just as smart.

An example of how a mistake can impact on a business comes from the export market at Pacific Direct; it's also useful in showing how stressful situations can be overcome. My husband Charlie was in charge of our first shipment of goods to the new export market of Croatia. He had diligently visited Croatia, quoted, sampled, followed through the sales process and had won a significant purchase order for goods to be sea-freighted to the country.

Imagine our devastation when we discovered that the freight company had shipped the goods onto a freight vessel going to *Korea* – completely misunderstanding the instruction to load goods onto a Croatian consolidated line. Because of the delay caused by the time taken to retrieve the products from the other side of the world we lost ongoing business, but we were able to sell the goods by discounting them heavily. The loss of profit was not nearly as painful as losing the time invested in developing the relationship – and a potentially considerable client.

You cannot say that it does not matter how such a mistake happened. It does – so that you can develop a system to double-check and avoid a repeat of such a nightmare. The real pain was that a great deal of time had to be spent on correcting the error, but there was no point in initiating a witch hunt. The paperwork had been right, and all that happened was that the freight company guy loading the goods had misread the instructions and put our products in the wrong box. For the record, despite this whole mess the buyer then reordered as he was impressed by the way we had dealt with the disastrous situation and kept him informed throughout the process of putting things right. That's proof that great relationships can be developed by putting mistakes right – possibly even more than by having a perfect delivery process in the first place.

Go for it

Progress will not come from staying within your comfort zone. Put yourself in challenging, new, often initially uncomfortable situations and push your boundaries all the time. Set bigger goals than you might originally consider, go to places that you think are perhaps beyond your ability, contact people you may never have dreamed of meeting but who may give you time, and constantly challenge yourself to deliver beyond your greatest expectations.

Are you ready?

Here are a few thoughts to use and assess whether your company is ready for international trade.

- Do you have a euro or any other currency price list? If so, what coverage on exchange have you built into these product costs? It is unlikely you will sell into Europe without a euro offer, and you have to sell to the US in dollars except in exceptional circumstances.

- Are there any safety standards in the target market which would apply to your products? Are they compliant with them? What is the cost impact of making them compliant?

- Do you have a multilingual manual? One simple example of something that took time at Pacific Direct was the six language 'how to mount' manual for the dispenser system we sold to hold larger bottles of hand wash. This was very time consuming, and therefore costly.

- Respect other cultures. Our ability to make friends all over the world through the seventeen different languages that team Pacific could converse in was critical.

- Minimise the feel of a physical difference between you and a client abroad. We would be flexible with working hours for those staff involved in 'other markets'. If they found that being in the UK office later than normal allowed them to make better phone contact with hotels in a time-zone behind ours, then they worked later hours (actually people at Pacific worked many hours and this was a huge reason for our success). The value of sometimes making the right call at the right time of day can be the difference between success and failure in international growth. If your new market is awake during the middle of the night, are you?

International sales can be a really big challenge for any business and cannot be achieved generally as a one-man band – although, on reflection, this is what I did. My point is that when we took on larger-scale business at Pacific we bothered to train the receptionist and every other member of staff on how to handle incoming calls in the appropriate language: French for Sofitel, for instance. You have to be more responsive when convincing someone to buy from another country and these small efforts made a huge difference to our likelihood of success.

Getting there...

Should you wish to discover more about the possibility of expanding to an export market, the cheapest way these days is to get on a plane and visit it. Here you will find a list of suggestions to pre-plan your trip to make it as useful as possible and some 'in country' hints and tips for maximising your success on arrival.

Prior to visiting a new marketplace it is necessary to make sure that your time will be utilised fully while there, so the more research that is done prior to visiting, the more cost-effective the actual trip. Here are some questions you should be asking yourself.

- Do I have appointments arranged which may lead to orders? Aim for eight solid appointments each day – some of these may only be catalogue drop-offs, pre-prepared the night before. In a strange place, it is interesting and fun getting around and, after all, if you maximise your exposure and opportunity potential you may have a good reason to come back. You should have a target sales figure in mind which more than covers the cost of exploration and market research. Here is a clever way of appearing slightly more sizable than you are – have your PA (a luxury I could not afford in the early days, and you could do this yourself) fax or email in advance of your global tour announcing your arrival days and availability. This shows that your time is limited and, when done in advance of trips, it is a powerful way of filling up your diary.
- Do my products require any particular licences or special paperwork for importation into a new market?
- Are there any barriers to entry? If so, what are they?
- Are there any leading suppliers native to the particular marketplace that have monopolies?
- What is the customer's response to the potential of my visit?
- Is my industry in growth or decline within this market?
- Is there financial stability? Are there any potentially difficult currency issues?
- Is there a sample tax? For example, two of the islands in the Caribbean have a US$400 sample tax, which you have to pay in order to take samples and brochures in.

- Will there be adequate mobile coverage? Will there be facilities for email or fax? Check to see if communications are OK.
- Should staff security issues be reviewed?

If these questions point to a negative and unprofitable outlook, then a trip to that particular marketplace may not be viable. If the answers are positive and the market looks encouraging, the next path would be to contact various organisations who can help. I have always found asking for assistance and advice easy. You are meant to be able to get assistance from government funding and organisations, and of course these days there is a huge amount of information – and useful check lists – available online on any subject you care to imagine. So use these sources, they will save you hours of pointless thinking and planning and allow you to concentrate on content and adding value.

The UK Trade and Industry Department is a massive and helpful resource in this area; searching online for 'exporting' will lead you to them. The British Embassy or High Commission in the area you are planning to visit is another potentially good contact and, providing the right questions are asked, useful information can be obtained from them too. This assistance can cost, however. The fees for some of the work may seem expensive, and frankly I think there are lots of ways of avoiding this cost, but your industry may not be quite as obvious as hospitality. The time and effort this could save might well pay dividends.

You may also be a member of a business organisation – such as the Entrepreneurs Organisation (www.entrepreneurs.org) – which could help, and if you are not, then membership is certainly something you should consider. The international spread of other entrepreneurs can shortcut your way to local knowledge and locally important contacts in a priceless fast-track way. I never made enough use of this but was always overwhelmed by the generosity of time and information such like-minded near-strangers gave.

From talking to the relevant organisations you may find that there is an independent body which will liaise with you more closely, as these independents are more concerned with the growth and development of the country by expanding suppliers and looking for alternative import markets. For example, CARITAG is the Caribbean Trade Advisory Group to British Trade International. You may find that these independent bodies will give you people to talk to who perhaps have been exporting for several years to your chosen market, and this will give you real information.

Do note that the above process is all about contacting, faxing, emailing, talking to the right people and finding out what is available for you to use. Make sure you leave plenty of time and allow for communication problems and lazy replies.

The advantages of forward planning:
- Orders can be placed more quickly from prospects gathered in advance.
- Time will be spent in actual 'contact' time whilst there.
- Arranging the itinerary logically may save costs in flights.

As a cost-effective business person in a new market area you should have looked into:
- The best flight deal.
- The best accommodation package. Make sure your hotel caters for the business traveller, especially if the market area is a typical holiday destination. Additional costs can creep up due to email and faxing charges if the hotel is not geared towards the business market.
- Transportation. Public transport is obviously the cheapest way to travel but may not be practical when carrying

samples. Car hire is by far the best choice for getting lots done in a day. Taxis are fine for short journeys but are expensive and add to bottom-line costs. And study a map before you travel; if you have a few appointments in one day make sure the locations are close enough to be practical, however you travel.

■ Find out if there are any public holidays or special events – for example, cricket can make the Caribbean come to a standstill.

■ If samples and documents are sent in advance, allow plenty of time for them to clear customs; it may also be possible to include an express release letter.

■ Is there a local show/exhibition/event that you can link your trip to, in order to maximise exposure?

■ If you are attending an exhibition, remember that exhibition companies have a lot of planning information available, so use it.

You also need to consider cultural respect and the value of language. Do not underestimate the value of a small amount of effort put into learning foreign terms and simple words and phrases. Take a genuine interest in the country you are visiting and the people in it, and your opportunities will unfold.

Whilst there:
■ Use Yellow Pages and other business directories. Look through the directories and make sure you are familiar with the relevant businesses in your market. Look at other sections too; so for Pacific that would have meant looking at tourism organisations, construction companies, hotel and catering equipment suppliers. Make a call to a few and explain what you are doing in the market.

Incidentally, suppliers who are already established in the location may also want to see you – firstly to find out what products you are selling, but also to find out whether you are going to threaten their business. So be very clear and keep things open.

■ Do some shopping. Try to visit possible outlets which offer your type of products in the market, if relevant. You may find local manufacturers, and you will also get an understanding about where the products (again, you need to generalise beyond your business) are being imported from or manufactured. If you can find out and it looks worthwhile, try to get an appointment. You never know, you may find a new supplier for your business; however, the likelihood is that you will gain greater understanding of what you are up against.

■ Don't forget confirmations. Double-check your appointments, and try to arrange more. If you have made the effort to travel, people do tend to be more approachable and may make the effort to see you.

■ Talk to taxi drivers. This may sound a little odd, but the information taxi drivers hold is unbelievable. If you find a taxi driver who is good, take a card and use him again. They tend to have little gems of useful information.

There are some additional points to consider, too. Firstly, not everyone in the world is a workaholic, and working times abroad can be quite different. Certain areas of the world are very laid back and the working day may finish at 3 or 4 p.m. – though the normal start could be 7 a.m. Try to find this out prior to your trip, so you can plan your time carefully.

Another good idea is to write a daily diary, including who you have met, contact names and details, information you have found out. Business cards can come in handy but a daily diary makes you remember much more. It can also be helpful back in the office, so that both the office and you are communicating. Depending on the day, it should be easy to write out in about half an hour. Take thorough notes on your enquiry sheets, too; fill out all the information you think you could possibly need. And don't forget to get enquiries back to the office as soon as you can in an easy format to understand – this way, quotations can be sent out more quickly on your return and your business will look more efficient.

Always ask, ask, ask. In every appointment, try to find out what people find hard to source, whether they have delivery problems, all the additional questions. A foot in the door, with branded pens, may lead to business later. Give people your email address, and let them know that you can be contacted for the remainder of your trip in case they forget something. Make them aware that you are approachable. And finally, always discuss your terms and conditions of trading in detail, with a great focus – and an open conversation – on payment terms and trade timing. Too often a customer may really love a product but the trading terms they are offered negate any real interest. In most cases you will have to match or beat the service terms of a current supplier.

You need to think about freight, too. To get the best rates, shop around. When visiting a country that you are likely to export to, and perhaps where you will require import services following sales, always find out who are the top players in the freight industry and where possible make face to face appointments with them. Do your usual supplier diligence but also ask the people you meet and the customers you service how freight works for them and which services they prefer.

Getting the finances right

The financial side of trading abroad must be considered; it is vital to your business. If you are going to become an international trader you need to be very aware of the strength of your banking partners as you develop wider demands and deal with endless currency transactions and challenges. Every international bank has guides and publications on each country you may wish to trade in. Get them; they are both free and useful.

Be very aware that outside the UK your contracts are worthless, so getting payment for your goods is everything – selling is only part of the proposition. Only deliver once you have the money, or when you have cast-iron terms of trading such as a letter of credit drawn on a reputable bank. Learn the value of the use of letters of credit to grow your business by having your bank explain them to you. Then, working with your client in partnership, perfect between you the exact details of the letter of credit *before* presentation to the bank. Never do these negotiations through the bank as every change costs money; in fact, do not go to your bank until you are completely happy with the definitions of terms. And always say no to business that will not pay on your terms. My first slippery customer was in Russia. It took literally months for money transfers to be made, but the orders were sizable – and were only actually made when the money was in my bank.

One final note: of course, there are boundaries and restrictions, and common sense should apply when travelling to some countries. I've been lucky; in the soap-sales world there has been no need to travel to war zones. There are also some territories where a man will still be better received than a woman, but times are changing and I have only ever felt disadvantaged by being female in Saudi Arabia. Only once did I ever feel unsafe on my solitary travels, and that was arriving in Mexico City at 2 a.m. and having to find a cab at a deserted airport. It was only a momentary fear and I have found that with luck, a solid composure and outward confidence much can be achieved.

Lara's laws

- It's more enjoyable, less stressful and frankly more fun to work eighteen hours a day when you are away from your family.
- Pre-planning, with targeted success, ensures you focus on maximising your potential.
- Reduce time wasted in follow-up by utter clarity during face to face meetings to ensure you have not wasted your efforts.
- After-trip follow-up is paramount. Plan time to make sure this happens before you return to your daily routine chaos, or the momentum of your trip is wasted.

7
Cut once and cut deep: the tough times

Chapter goals

- Your demonstrable actions in setting new strategic directions depends on great communication and consistency of behaviour. Stop doing some things and delegate them to others – it's a powerful starting point.
- The importance of decisive but fair action during challenging economic times can rescue your potential.
- Measurements can sometimes present you with surprising results. The importance of target setting to focus activity is vital.

Right up to the time I went to Cranfield, I had no idea about the success or exceptional growth we had achieved at Pacific. We now had a global business platform – small, but nevertheless global. Our own toiletries manufacturing plant in China was in the first of several locations and we had, nearly simultaneously, bought a 51 per cent share holding in Wisam S.p.o.l. in the Czech Republic. So by 1998, I owned a fledging factory in China and two weeks later suddenly owned a going concern in the Czech Republic. It wasn't the way I'd planned to do things, but it was certainly a risk worth taking. Did I have time to do thorough numbers, analysis and feasibility? No. Did I employ well reputed, competent but outrageously expensive lawyers? Yes. I am proud to say that by then we also had licences for brands such as Neutrogena, and this particular one was quite an accomplishment, given that this was the first time Johnsons had been convinced to sub-license their brand to a little-known English hotel amenities company.

We had achieved extraordinary growth and were becoming recognised amongst the competition. I had gone through my personally most unhappy phase of the business and, following completion of the Cranfield programme, had a new lease of life. I had started the course with grave concerns about the business being undercapitalised, poorly managed and without a plan. I started to put these things right. Having been pulled in every direction and feeling out of control, I handed over the general management of the business as fast as I could. Meanwhile I concentrated on funding, focused growth and business development in a much more rigorous way to fit our newly defined niche strategy. The massive turning point that introduced new strategic focus could not have been delivered without a monumental effort to delegate more and better, and change my own daily habits and focus considerably. This was not easy, but it was imperative; without consistent effort on my part we would never have established new foundations for growth.

When I left Cranfield, 56 per cent of our turnover was from sales of non-licensed branded products – 'house lines' – and we sold across a complete breadth of hotel types from one star and caravans all the way through to the Dorchester. We serviced many diverse environments, from Travelodge to the newly opening Great Eastern Hotel. And during my time at Cranfield we had started bidding for our biggest potential new business – Accor Hotels-owned Sofitel Hotels, for worldwide provision of their guest accessories. This was a hugely significant, even business changing, piece of business. The Sofitel contract placed huge demands on cash management. The significant impact that it would have – and the risk that was attached, due to the global nature of deliveries – was a challenge for the business. At a board meeting we took a vote following a presentation of the pros and cons of taking on the contract, and I will never forget the passion with which I presented the case for taking on the risk of servicing Sofitel in fifty-seven countries, often in French, and delivering to over 130 hotels at launch.

Things get serious...

And then 9/11, SARS and foot and mouth virtually destroyed the company in its tenth year of existence.

The impact these disasters had on travel was enormous – during 2001, after the World Trade Center bombing occurred, we had key clients plummet from 88 per cent occupancy to a mere 6 per cent, and I travelled on a flight from London to Dubai the following month with only six other passengers. I believe that the relentless desire I have to learn from others and continually challenge the status quo enabled us to survive this period, one which could have been fatal to many businesses.

We also had problems with our US operation which added to our difficulties. I wanted to attract someone with real industry knowledge who could accelerate our introduction and potential success in the US marketplace, but by employing the person I chose I significantly upset another company, a major player. I was sued for US$1 million, which was a new level of seriousness given the fact that our finances were stretched and we were working at a phenomenal pace. What I did not know then is that any business can sue another company in the US for sometimes spurious reasons – and they can do this as an anti-competitive tactic, to slow down new entrants to a market. The scale of legal costs can be enough of a deterrent for many businesses to back off. I felt strongly (knowing we had done nothing wrong) that we should fight our corner, though the task of fighting a litigation issue in a foreign land was sizable. I did as I always do in situations when I am out of my depth, and approached people I thought would be in the know and asked for help; as usual, I received it. We eventually settled after the deposition, and our costs were paid. All of these problems caught up with us and we entered a hideous period during 2003.

I used a 'cut once and cut deep' strategy to save the company, and had to make a third of the global team redundant. I developed a formula for deciding which team members had to go and who had to stay. It was a highly emotional situation but I managed my way out of it and learnt lots of lessons in the process.

We developed a skills rating system (see www.company shortcuts.com/documents) to create a fair and constructive methodology for how we would select the people who would stay and those we would have to make redundant. As a management group, we devised a score which reflected each individual's ability in each section of the business (you will have to rely on multitasking individuals for the best recovery from any staff reduction). We recognised that there could be swing decisions following discussions, and ultimately the direct manager of an individual led the final score set. When this process was applied, it became rather surprising how people who previously seemed to be singular in their contribution were actually far more useful when times were tough and an 'all hands on deck' approach was required.

We spent several days rigorously inputting our knowledge of each employee in the company and argued the point on an individual's character, attitude and likely ability to work doubly hard even when paid less. It was a hideous situation, which I never intend to repeat – but it is one which, I am sure, applies to any small company in the light of a dramatic downturn in business. A similar process may ensure you live to fight another day.

I need not go into the nightmare of running a redundancy process within UK law. Three weeks of consultancy; endless legal advice; cost and sense-checking the process. There were horrible face to face discussions with members of the team desperately trying to prove their worth and, worst of all, telling friends that I was putting them out of a job despite how unbelievably loyal, hard-working and capable they were.

It is a memorable lesson in human nature how differently individuals will react during times of stress. Overall I can only be filled with pride and admiration for the good grace that so many staff applied to the situation, and some people I made redundant came back to work for us when business improved. I guess this shows that if you run a decent and open process, you protect assets for future re-employment. The way you treat people will be remembered for much longer than you will ever believe.

The most dreadful part of the whole redundancy process was the day – after a four week consultancy period according to British law – when I sat with each and every member of the team in the UK and let them know whether they would be retained or released. By the end of the day I was physically and mentally exhausted, and even stopped on the way home to cry my eyes out in a layby, but I also knew that the worst was over – and the next day we could start rebuilding.

Remotivation

In my experience, it is not emotionally rewarding being the CEO of a company so don't expect it to be so. Of course, there may be exceptional days when no one resigns, no one announces that they are pregnant, no one puts in a petty complaint and everyone is performing to their maximum ability, with systems and processes aligned. It is often lonely and scary, and there will be unrelenting demands for you to be cheerful and positive. If you cannot overwhelmingly assure yourself that you can fake it in the tough times, then how can you expect others to buy into and believe in your positive ambitions?

Some of the really meaningful things that I took away from Cranfield helped me during this period. Exceptionally valuable was the importance of target setting. From goal setting to writing down actions (endless lists of things to do), I have seen people consistently achieve things they originally felt were insurmountable challenges. By measuring performance against goals I too have managed to progress, and looking to yourself can get you through the challenges.

What might you gain from self-setting goals?
- Greater self-confidence to push you further – and make it a habit.
- Independence.
- An understanding of your own strengths and weaknesses and how to overcome these – or delegate accordingly.

- That through tenacity and persistence you will be an enabler for things you want to happen, things which will not happen without action.
- You will open up a world of choices and opportunities.

You can apply the principle to both small and large goals. I endlessly wrote down – and still do – things that occurred to me that I wanted to improve. Ideas continually creep into my mind which will be forgotten without a scribble for reference, and I even had 'get it done today' notepads printed to help others in the company adopt this habit. It does not matter where (to some extent) you capture your thinking, but your thoughts will be much more likely to be realised when you write them down.

Through success you will breed more success. You will build momentum and your choice to act and change something is only going to come from changing something *now*. It would be delusional to think that no one carries any baggage but, having attended a life-coaching course and courses on planning and self-development, I am endlessly horrified by the lack of confidence some individuals have.

Having a go is critical, as is changing the status quo – walk tall, even when you may not have all the courage of your convictions; fake it and you will go far. If you believe that anything is possible, have a plan and action points, consciously focus on your goals, you will grow and gain freedom and deserve to get everything you desire. It is your choice, so change what you are doing and you will get a different result. If you do not change, then do not be disappointed.

Another powerful tool that allowed me to get through the tough times which I learnt from Dale Carnegie was to ask myself, 'What's the worst thing that could happen?' Having established either that being at the bottom of a problem meant the only way was up, or that there was usually someone worse off than myself, I would count my blessings, take a deep breath, and then crack on.

Learning organisations and the importance of continual self-growth

In much of my business development I was rather slow on the uptake, and one of my lost opportunities in the early days was not being involved in some kind of entrepreneurs' club. It would have helped me talk to others about the topics which are daily challenges to most businesses.

Since I learnt the benefit of this kind of independent and unbiased advice – from the experience of other people – I have benefited more than I can say. You can find other people's ideas energising, simply bigger, annoying, a great sense check, or just comforting at times of loneliness, and it is worth everyone exploring these kinds of opportunities. It is important that you build your own network of help and support advice – and unbiased input – from people who you respect and value. This group of individuals will change and grow as your business has new development demands. Always respect the time and effort individuals will give and try, wherever possible, to pay people back with information exchange and shared learning, perhaps with introductions and links to progress.

Networking the hell out of meetings needs to be handled correctly, but I have never found that time I have given others in mentoring has not been paid back. Short cutting introductions and having access to recommended experts from successful people will speed your own potential to stay ahead of the game. Relentless record keeping of such meetings is an effort worth making, and again something I should have done better. I have not been diligent enough to build my own database of contacts with fuller information. This is disappointing and will be disadvantageous, so do not make the same mistakes as I have. Never undervalue the record you keep of any and all contacts you make in the progression of your business; these may be priceless relationships further down your path. So start now.

Onwards

In between the challenges of the launch of Sofitel and the company survival mode of making cuts in all areas of the business, one thing I continued to focus on was my utter belief in what we were offering. Once the hotel industry recovered from the endless run of disasters, which were not of its own making, I was certain that brand luxury toiletries could become the norm.

We continually invested in better brochure presentations of our brands, continually looked for better ways to promote our offer uniquely whilst educating the marketplace in the trends we were leading. Given the redundancies that we had made, we had to have something positive to say. We trained, communicated and trained again the message of what was the core company offering as a whole. Exciting momentum started to build as we recovered from our own hospitality recession and moved into a period of accelerated success.

Lara's laws

■ Change is the norm for a growing business. You and your team have to embrace change to maximise your potential. Set these foundations early as a bedrock of your culture, and you can survive anything.

■ Commitment comes from self-belief when you know what is right for the business. This is your own inner drive; don't expect external support.

■ It is better to make hideous redundancy decisions and see them through fairly, than it is to die slowly through endless small cuts. Small cuts will not establish a platform for growth.

■ Applied learning counts. The courage of your convictions will be recognised and, even when times are bad, people who are treated with respect will remain loyal assets.

8

If at first you don't succeed, try and try again

Chapter goals

- Be clear about the massive, relentless commitment to running a company in fast growth. Time is money, so apply yourself to the profitable stuff.
- Excellence in negotiation is important. And not just your own, but excellence embedded within the culture of the whole business.
- Don't be afraid of the big opportunities; be persistent, professional and different.
- Set outstanding standards in personal organisation so that others can follow your example. The more efficient you and your team are, the more profitability takes care of itself.

Apparently one definition of an entrepreneur is that of someone who is a taker of risks. I would suggest, however, that most entrepreneurs do not directly feel they are doing this. They feel they are innovating, challenging a normal process with the aim of improvement – usually for the customer and for themselves – and their expectation is that they will be rewarded with success by challenging a status quo and never accepting 'no' for an answer.

Challenging the normal way of doing things is without doubt a trait I see in every successful entrepreneur. They will recount stories about how they have always broken the rules, boast about detentions at school and will – like me, I suspect – enjoy the process of beating any system. There may well be an element of nervous anticipation in beating a system in competition and gaining the advantage by wit and determination with a bit of brain power. This kind of highly exhilarating result is the addiction of business improvement and something to be recommended. You should have a Plan B – of sorts – or at least be good enough/fast enough/flexible enough/intelligent enough to change should Plan A not deliver the required results. But if you don't try it, you will never know.

I strongly suggest that unless you are prepared for new challenges daily (sometimes changes lined up every minute and coming one after the other, and all seeming larger than any before) – and unless you have the ability to believe that you can always take something positive away from any experience – then you are the wrong person to grow a business. You will need to move outside your comfort zone, to operate in an area outside the normal parameters of what you have previously experienced.

I have a natural and relentless wish to do new things, a belief that 'anything is possible' – and it is. I continually wish to try new approaches and challenge the status quo at every turn. I want to be doing whatever I am doing now faster, better, bigger and always more profitably, and I think anyone can develop this drive to their financial or life benefit.

Time is money and hence everything has a calculated value. I have already mentioned that I hope that you have a rough idea of your hourly value for everything you and your team players do, and that you apply this accordingly. If you cannot see yourself increasing the value of whatever the enterprise you are working in, then find something more profitable where you can. As soon as I began this endless questioning of my daily activities I gave up doing the 'small stuff' and made incremental changes, delegating as much as possible to other people so that I could grow new ventures. It is a serious pain to map your minutes during the day, but I am only suggesting you do it for a week, though some lawyers and accountants do it all their working lives. In just a week you can discover what you really spend your time doing, make adjustments and then do what you really *should* be doing. Do what you are good at and do it really well. Enjoy doing your job and always employ other people, with better skills than you, to do the stuff you know someone else will do better.

I accept that in constantly taking on challenges I will, from time to time, fail. It is important to learn the need to fail and bounce back, and learn it quickly. Always look at the positive side of failure and, more importantly, celebrate and share the lessons you learn from failure with as many people as you possibly can. The value you will create from endless sharing of your own fallibility (learn to laugh at yourself), the more you can expect others to feel safe when doing the same. If you can develop an organisation where mistakes are OK – not lacking in consequences, but certainly not frowned upon – the faster your business will achieve your goals. The more mistakes you and others make, the more likely you will be increasing the successful resilience and experience of your business. And these value-adding experiences will accelerate your chances of success.

Going with your guts

Sometimes you have to make a decision to go with your gut feeling. You may feel uncomfortable, even odd, but if you learn to translate the nervous anticipation of your guts you will, in my experience, not be let down. Ultimately, I acted when things made sense – when I felt I had done enough homework to make a sensible judgement and when the gut feeling was right. Of course, the scale of impact of some decisions will change and become substantial, but it is amazing how experience allows these decisions to meld one into another. Keep practising on applying decisions and making mistakes and you will find it very hard later on to remember all the setbacks. Not dwelling on these becomes easy. I do appreciate that I am lucky in that I never had the shackles of obligation brought on through running a family firm (often a huge honour, I am sure). You will be surprised how comfortable you become acting on instinct the faster you can overcome hurdles and the sooner those around you take on their own challenges.

Sometimes you do not have the luxury of time to research, reference or do your own normal risk analysis. Opportunity lost due to inaction is a painful and slow way to grow a successful enterprise. Of course, weigh up the possibilities, go in with your planned expected outcome, have a back-up plan – but move things forward nevertheless. Don't forget that sometimes there is a perfect halfway house which will buy you time to think, as that can be priceless. What is not an option is endless procrastination – like the one challenging problem that sits in your in-tray for an interminable time. I can assure you that the challenge is always half the size it seemed, takes half the time to resolve and gives double the satisfaction if conquered earlier in the day. If you practise using your guts in everything you do, you really can claim to be taking calculated risks. This does not mean you cannot change your mind when a plan is not working. A great strength can be to admit failure and cut your losses – and earlier admission may save you a fortune. Do remember, too, that running a business can't all be down to calculated risk, and that sometimes the time will be right for you to take a much more deliberate decision. Clearly, as your business gets bigger and with numbers increasing, more calculations are required – but that doesn't mean you should stay in your comfort zone.

The comfort zone of chasing money (and getting paid) can make or break a company. As I've said, I am continually amazed at how poorly companies do this. The basics are just the minimum standard in collections. If you did the work, carried out your promise to contract, then you are owed the money, and you should feel strongly about getting what you are worth. Fast and efficient collection keeps a company's options open, keeps cash under your own control and will constantly give you opportunities for new development. Never lose sight of what you are owed, by when and by whom.

Here is a good example of extreme collections that still makes me smile today. Pacific Direct were owed the equivalent of over a year's salary by a company in Oman which had been allowed a shipment of goods without receipt of funds – a mistake by a new member of the team who had not had the correct training on our international payment terms. After diligently chasing these funds from the UK and being promised pleasantly and often that the funds would be transferred, I had the opportunity to visit Oman from nearby Dubai and collect our money in person. I had previously worked in the Gulf States at Yellow Pages, so I knew the power of being a physical money collector. I had weighed up the pros and cons and thought I could play this role to my advantage.

Together with an inexperienced female colleague, but without an appointment, I flew to Oman and took a taxi directly to the client's office from the airport. We entered the building and I disregarded the receptionist other than to ask if the Financial Director concerned was in, and then we strode on. In those days the offices of most companies in the Middle East had individual rooms, with large titles and names outside the doors to signify the importance of the inhabitant. We found the Finance Director in the process of packing up for the day, but sat down by his large desk and introduced ourselves with as much confidence as we could muster. I showed him the copy invoice and asked why my bill had been ignored continually and when I might be paid. I knew he had the power to decide to pay the bill immediately should he choose to do so.

The Finance Director was caught unawares, and immediately stretched towards the phone, explaining that he would have to ask someone for the money to be paid. In response I explained, reasonably calmly, that should he either make a call or cause a fuss, we would refuse to leave. I knew he would not wish to embarrass his boss by having two women in situ in his office, and this was where we struck lucky. The boss was still in the building and the Finance Director suggested that perhaps he should take me to the perpetrator of my problem. We were invited into a large boardroom where I explained my woes and was indeed promised immediate settlement of the invoice – which we then took as an irrevocable cash payment. Did I enjoy the experience? Not at the time. Was it entirely outside anything I had ever expected to do? Absolutely. Was I within my rights? I think so – and we did get the money.

Inertia is not an option

Endless planning is not advisable, but calculated planning can be important. Planning will still not always get you to the end result you target, though.

The most simple and effective planning source I have found is a piece of paper. You need some quiet time to think, then divide the paper into two and write down pros and cons on either side of the page. In bigger decisions you may need to weight the topics, but this method has progressed many a decision I have made when approached openly. Too many people spend too much time thinking far too much about which direction to go in, but at least a mistaken direction results in a reduced number of options for your next move. Preparation can prevent poor performance but you'd be excited, amazed and exhilarated by the brilliance achieved by simply having a go.

Please do not suggest the SMART (specific, measured, achievable, realistic, timely) working habit. Although I agree entirely that targets set should be established within these simple parameters, and that SMART working makes for greater efficiency, it is not the be-all and end-all it is sometimes assumed to be. It is all very well people telling me that the more intelligently I work the more successful I may become; I cannot argue this point. The point I can argue is that – given the intention to always be in the lead, always striving to be better than the rest, and always striving to work as 'smartly' as possible – the more hours I put in, the more quickly I would convert my dream into cash. I have worked hideously hard, and I see this as the investment I put in to getting where I wanted to go faster than others whom simply did not put in the time. Too many people 'think' they work hard, 'think' they are dedicated to their businesses. But it is a fact that too many of them have not milked every moment to create their success and, worse still, do not apply maximum focus. Some personal sacrifices are mandatory; lead by example.

It is OK to dream but you must focus on reality. I was once told what dream stands for:

- D = Desire. Most people run a business to make a difference or provide a solution.
- R = Reasons. You are passionate about what you are doing and have clarity of vision, a determination to succeed.
- E = Enthusiasm. This is required in bucketloads, in order to keep plugging on. Some people fall at this hurdle, and pursuing something which is not working is wasted time. Knowing when to walk away is easier said than done, though.
- A = Actions. These are utterly critical to business progression and in most cases speed matters.
- M = Manifestations. This is the behavioural aspect of success; what was critical for me was the pride in knowing we had great products and delivered on our promise.

I am by no means a perfectionist. In fact, I generally loathe perfectionists. I do not believe they are usually cost-effective in running a business, as the time wasted in aiming to develop what in one person's perspective is important is only going to be changed by someone else. Get the message out, get it out in a format that the majority can understand, and take action; do not procrastinate. Business is often won by those who are in the market working, creating and reacting to opportunities – not by those working on how to get started. Indian corner-shop owners who open long hours deserve their success, for example. So, where possible, I do not employ many perfectionists. I am certain perfectionists have their place, but I just cannot bear time-wasting effort when I could be selling more to as many customers as possible. Having said that, I have employed and been privileged to work with individuals with awesome capabilities in attention to detail – people who have been utterly priceless in the application of their skills in protecting our company. But not, though, in sales roles.

Going the extra mile in sales

In the early days I used to train our sales people in the available hours of the decision-makers in our business. We discussed their most accessible times – indeed we asked the customers continually when was the best time to approach them – and we respected and made the most of any such opportunity. (Hotel housekeepers, for example, tend to stop for a coffee around 11 a.m. – an ideal moment.)

Your own industry may be used to certain style of delivery. It may be comfortable, but if you can give a better service for no additional cost then move your clients to a better comfort zone. They will buy from you for the value you bring. On a personal note, have you dedicated yourself to selling all the hours of the day and banning yourself from administration/ emails and any kind of written work and follow-up quotes until after sales hours? Do this with utter dedication and your success rate will increase.

Scary big clients do not exist

If you have a major client that you are scared of reaching out to, call them and keep calling them until you speak to them. Your persistence will pay off. Call at different times of the day or on different days, and always leave a sensible, confident message with an engaging challenge. Any conversation with a stranger can be challenging, so why not aim for the top of any organisation?

Ideas for reaching the 'impossible to reach'

■ Send them something far more interesting than the normal and expected glossy brochure, perhaps something entertaining. I once sent a buyer a tube of Savlon – he had explained that if he supported my prices his management would beat him up. I pointed out on the accompanying compliment slip that I could not help with the prices, as they were value for money, but that perhaps I could help him recover from the beating.

■ Remember that you are just one of a myriad of voices in pursuit of a sale. I find there is nothing more boring than a repetitive pitch without imagination, and I've been on the receiving end of many since the sale of Pacific Direct. People who asked from the outset whether the call was convenient made an immediately good impression by putting me first.

■ Do you make it utterly simple for people to contact you? Are all your contact details on all the communications stuff you send out? Do you text new customers these details immediately after a first conversation to make their lives easier?

■ Have you networked and attended dinners in your industry to meet the power players? Have your worked your socks off to get other customers to reference you to their contacts? Introductions like these are priceless.

■ Make sure you leave energising, interesting and compelling voice messages. Be more entertaining than the rest, and more approachable.

- When you meet your 'hard to reach' target don't forget to:
  - smile,
  - speak in a confident voice and change your tone to suit the person you are speaking to,
  - be enthusiastic in whatever you say or ask,
  - maintain good eye contact,
  - offer a firm handshake,
  - be sincere – you can't fake friendliness,
  - stand tall, and
  - have a manner that communicates the expectation that you deserve and expect to get what you request.

So get organised, get dedicated and get calling.

Dealing with challenging situations

I suspect I learnt my confidence in getting more for any inconvenience I was caused from my mother, who would take me with her whilst she did things like returning imperfect fruit to the grocer. It also taught me to get real value for money.

If you are uncomfortable with a service provider, do your homework and change them – but do not make the change until you have done your preparation, and always express your unhappiness with the incumbent supplier so you give them a chance to compete. You'd be amazed at how a comparative quote – and you can fudge this bit – can get someone to sharpen their pencil. We did this relentlessly when buying freight for clients (we passed on the freight costs, with proof of quotes).

You may not like these challenging conversations, but you are going to need some mettle to ensure that you run the leanest cost base possible. It is a fact that in order to be the best provider you do not have to be the cheapest – but if you are the best-run company with the lowest overhead, you will have far more flexibility in tough times. You must, irrespective of your offer and positioning, always look to be the lowest-cost buyer: for example, team members at Pacific Direct shopped around relentlessly for the best value flights, lowest-cost hotel stays and any methods of saving money in every area. The importance of learning the ability to buy better should be trained throughout every company from accounts, who negotiate best currency transaction rates, through to sales. Each department of a company has to make purchases, and as a business gets bigger more people will need to have budget control and make spending decisions. Make sure you have a culture and education system that takes negotiation training to all parts of your company. You will save a fortune, and you cannot do it all yourself.

My own personal objective was perhaps more driven by a fear of failure – a great reason for constantly pushing the boundaries to get to my end goal faster. Overcoming the inertia of making no decision at all is easy when you are relentlessly dissatisfied and constantly critical of yourself. I am not the only one who likes the knife-edge between success and failure, after all – and businesses gain value from people like us.

Willpower does have to overcome the fear and silences when you create opportunities to be outside your comfort zone. Simply put, you have to put your money where your mouth is. Sometimes – well, often – people will laugh at your ideas and dismiss them out of hand as impossible, and nothing makes me more likely to be motivated than being told something is not possible.

I learnt to love the buzz of quietly congratulating myself for doing something difficult as I charged down the street. I set myself endless goals and targets, with sometimes laughably small rewards for doing difficult things. I was by no means always successful, but I suspect I automatically think through Plan B and so subconsciously know there is always another direction to take if the first one fails. Being successful is getting back up from a fall, as my parents encouraged me to do when I was learning to ride a bike. Learning this is critical to the ongoing pushing of boundaries, which is the backbone of continued enjoyable learning in my opinion – overcoming new obstacles and enjoying the rewards of efforts and tests passed.

As I mentioned in passing earlier, I gave myself small rewards related to my performance. I found them effective, so be imaginative and think about what motivates you. Here are a couple more examples of the sort of things I did. They may seem somewhat odd, but they were priceless rewards to me at the time:

■ Getting my legs waxed during office hours may not appeal to all, but having the time to do this was wonderful. The fact that I might have been on my phone talking to people throughout was something I never gave away. A double treat was turning off the phone for these few minutes.

■ If I managed to drill through my whole list of things to do whilst in the air on long-haul flights I would occasionally allow myself the treat of watching just one movie. (This was always difficult, as I learnt to sleep as soon as I relaxed – so the staying awake part of this treat often eluded me.)

I have been unable to think about this without laughing at myself, and I now find it utterly farcical that this is how I behaved. There is, nevertheless, a serious benefit to the relentless focus on maximising productivity. Every second counted in the competition to be the best at what we did. I did not feel under undue pressure and enjoyed the little buzz out of successful days made even more successful by squeezing every ounce of time out of hours of input.

I would be on the phone making calls from literally the minute I left the house to the time I arrived at the office – probably starting the morning with China, then Hong Kong, then Dubai (sometimes Egypt) and then the Czech Republic. These would be followed by Germany and UK numbers until the USA's working day kicked in. Sometimes I even ended by calling China again. I ate, drank, and educated myself and others in my car on the way to and from meetings. Time spent with team members was always an opportunity for organised catch-up in all sorts of ways. We would carry a note pad, write actions and laugh a bit at the madness of it all. I have even been so busy that I did once manage to drive home without Tamsin, my then tiny baby daughter, who was happily sleeping in her removable car seat. I left the office, turned all the lights off, drove six miles – and on parking realised I was missing something. I returned to the office to find that Tamsin had not stirred.

Other than being utterly paranoid about the business as a whole (I think in a healthy, determined, ever-improving way), I remained dedicated to looking after myself as much as possible in the pursuit of happy days at work. Try and keep a happy face on, even on the tough days. These are some of my strategies; you may find they can help you too.

- Start the day positively every day.

- Don't make a habit of exhaustingly long days. Never go to bed with important or urgent matters outstanding. I do not work till the wee small hours (unless it's critical); if you do, something has gone wrong in planning. Rewrite your priority action list at the end of every day and give your brain a chance to wind down – my method was watching the news.

- Immediately someone else presents you with a problem, consider it an opportunity – this mindset itself drives solutions thinking.

- Drink loads of water – and try to avoid the mid-afternoon coffee-kick habit.

- Every day at Pacific Direct started with an inspirational quote, and I bought all sorts of things to provide the quote of the day. The small boosts and lateral thinking brought about by this were, I think, immeasurable. Try it.

- Overall I have always had an attitude of gratitude – in fact, I would take it further than this. I would say I have an overwhelming sense of optimism, though balanced with a street-wise scepticism. Seeing the plus side of everything will stand you in good stead.

- Never become complacent and you can guarantee new challenges each day. The complacent are soon overtaken; fun diminishes when you are not in the front.

Here are a few more time-saving efficiencies

- Laptop balance – the ability to work in any place, at any time, day or night is priceless, but you do need to recognise when your brain is at its best for working on the really important stuff.

- Turn your phone off, and not just in all meetings out of courtesy. Do it at times when you really need to get a job done. One of the best decisions I made at the point when I was working towards developing my management team was not to adopt the use of a BlackBerry. They all had them – but I said that I did not wish to be inundated with more emails and that if they really needed my input then ringing me up was the best way to ask questions. Your team will work out many more decisions between them if they do not have the fall-back of consulting a higher authority every time.

- Organisational brilliance will be required by anyone running a business to the best of their abilities. I read *The Organised Executive* by Stephanie Winston which gave me tools with which to reduce procrastination and avoidance, and also to stop doing repetitive tasks. You have to be very self-disciplined to adopt these new skills but the time you will gain through efficiency is immense.

- Make messages matter. Many people still make calls and do not leave messages. I cannot understand this; if you have a reason to call, then leave a message and make it a good quality message, clear and concise. Doing so will save you repeating yourself.

Multitasking and managing your time effectively is a huge asset. I learnt recently that motivation is a balance between pain and pleasure – and so is getting your hair done whilst reading the umpteenth copy of a licensing agreement, contracts or other endless pages of legal drivel. What else did I multitask? Meetings, and meeting flexibility for one thing. I shared (sometimes slightly adapted) meeting notes with clients and team members. I organised my emails into saved, pending and to do, and I only reviewed them three times a day (I closed the auto pop-up, which is a pointless timewaster and creates massive distraction from getting core quality work completed). Yes, I would sometimes shut my door to send out the rare message that I was not interruptible, but this usually happened when speaking to staff privately and often about emotionally charged issues. I always blocked time for returning phone calls when I knew I could be less productive, such as when I was likely to be standing on station platforms or waiting in airports for flights. I would also arrange meeting locations to reduce wasteful time in transit.

As the company grew I never booked my own flights, never arranged travel stuff and parking, and worked tirelessly to look for shortcuts and timesavers in everything I and others did. Sometimes I made mistakes, and one was not using airport parking valet services as I thought they were a luxury. I was wrong, and I make no apologies for repeating this once more: you really must work out your hourly rate of earning if you have not already done so, and decide as you grow what support services you need to maximise your earning capacity.

Lara's laws

- Time is indeed money. You need to work out possible outcomes fast, then plan and get out, whilst remaining focused on the prize — and have a rough Plan B for if things go wrong. Ultimately, get on with it.
- Work harder than you have ever worked before, because every hour of effort you put in will build your asset. With two equally smart people, and all other circumstances being equal, the person that acts faster gets there first.
- Prioritisation is an art, persistence of effort does pay dividends, but learn to put in permanent solutions from mistakes.

9

Staying grounded – and really valuing the importance of people power

Chapter goals

- People, people, people: the importance of people in and at the heart of any company success.
- How to build momentum for great expectations and outstanding results.
- The importance of celebrations – big, small, any type – to ensure your working environment is the best in your industry, keep your staff turnover low and get the maximum value from your recruits.
- The value of competitor knowledge and how you can profit from a strong reputation.

My parents brought me up to value every person, irrespective of their role in life. Each individual should be treated with respect – the amount you will gain from being reasonable with everyone, engaging and open-minded is priceless. I have found that I always gain through engaging with everyone from the bus driver to a hotel concierge, and not only in terms of enjoying the lonely days of travel more than I otherwise would have done. I have seen pointless and arrogant behaviour from horribly wealthy individuals who, in my opinion, are probably missing out on a great deal of the enjoyment I have gained from engaging with strangers all over the world.

CARE: commit with attitude, reality and empathy

The sum of all the parts is always greater than one individual – or how to show you care *and* get results.

People lie at the heart of every business success. It's important that they should be cared for, coached, encouraged, challenged and treated with respect. In my experience every individual has something unique to offer. And also, in my experience, the people I have had the pleasure to work with have always delivered beyond their own expectations when given the opportunity to do so.

I recognise that not everyone has been given the same head start or the confidence I have. I also know that, like me, no one is perfect. The combination of a grounded upbringing from the old-fashioned values I was brought up with and the experiences I gained from my early years abroad have enabled me to see the world as a very small place with bags of opportunity. I also knew from the outset that a team would build a valuable and sellable asset, unlike a one-man band. An individual cannot alone create lasting sustainable value in a company. One of my favourite quotes is, 'A team can build something amazing, an individual cannot.' Although this is not entirely true, there is no question that the sum of many brains has often produced, for me, much greater results, faster and with less possibility of risk.

I did not truly learn or perhaps test these CARE skills until I attended the Dale Carnegie evening course on the subject of leadership. We had by then started recruiting very regularly. I always felt out of my depth employing people – indeed, it still is somewhat of a surprise how well we did in this area. Certainly it is a testament to my 'do as you would be done by' upbringing.

I felt strongly that I needed to have more structure to the way I worked. All I ever did prior to that in terms of self-training was to relentlessly read books on business, always noting and acting on the things I found to make sense. I would also attend any and every event in the local area (ideally breakfasts and evening events, as eating into my sales day was not great). I would learn any and every subject related to business.

At one of these events on security in business I learnt a small but useful tip about the value of informing every person who joined the company how Pacific felt about theft, and doing so face to face. In my introductory 'Welcome to Pacific Direct' chat with every member of staff I always said that I would go the extra mile to give them whatever I could in samples and learning, but that any kind of theft was unacceptable and would be dealt with seriously. I left no one in any doubt about our intentions and this set firm ground rules for expected behaviour which became exceptionally important as the team grew. This tip may sound basic, but the percentage of people who take anything from stationery to cash out of a business is significant, and the proven reduction in theft through informing employees personally that theft is not acceptable is also massive. More importantly, communicating basic rights and wrongs reminds people from the outset of the high standards set within the organisation as a whole. Pacific was never run as a charity; we always worked for profit and we never deluded anyone that the business was in existence to make anything but money. The point we communicated was that all the players contributed in their way to the profit pot, and we had schemes and rewards that meant everyone shared in that success.

The other thing I think that my 'Welcome to Pacific Direct' conversation did was to very clearly state our ambitions and company mission, who I was and what I stood for, our work ethics and expectations – and the rewards which we would share in return for success. Do not undervalue the importance of such an exchange, but make sure your new team member also has the chance to ask questions and clarifications. It took me too long to realise, as time wore on and the business became well-known and successful, how nervous people were to meet 'the boss' and how much they valued the opportunity at the outset of their new careers.

I have numerous strategies for getting the best from individuals – actually for getting individuals to get the most they can from themselves. You cannot underestimate the power of a clear vision, purposeful mission and clarity of direction when the team behind all the strategy move with engaged, energised and positive activity. Our welcome talk was an important part of this, and you will find a summary of what it covered on page 151.

I would immediately try and put individuals at ease, but this was one of the few meetings I would have with my desk firmly between the new recruit and myself; I needed to set the positioning for our relationship. By the end of the meeting I would be on my feet passionately talking about potential and rewards and breaking down the barriers as I would inform the new person that if my door was open (as it was most of the time) then anyone and everyone was welcomed in.

Incidentally, do not underestimate the power and meaning of a well-timed, well-composed and appropriately expressed 'thank you'. I have found some of the most powerful thanks I gave were in the quietest times, often the toughest times of our business growth. These are the times when people can be found working late, going the extra mile in setting up an exhibition stand, or producing exceptional work and results. I have gone out of my way to use this free tactic to score emotional loyalty points, which sounds manipulative (and it is) but I always did it with genuine meaning – and I began the welcome talk by thanking the employee for joining us.

'Welcome to Pacific Direct...'

Pacific Direct is a family-orientated company where I expect to get more than my pound of flesh; what I aim to do is have a team that gives willingly (pounds of flesh in terms of effort), and in return I would hope to make the experience enjoyable.

Training is the backbone of the company's success. The rules are that no one should join and be comfortable standing still. We all have skills to share to learn from each other; we all need to be learning to stay at the top of our game so that we can move on up, earn more and as a result give others the chance to step up also.

Pacific is a place where people should be encouraged to have fun whilst delivering outstanding customer service – always remember that the customer pays our salaries and that ultimately without them we have nothing.

Honesty is the best policy. We have a luxury approach to the market where we expect all the team members to pull in the same direction – towards big, established year goals – and that therefore taking anything from the company is a serious offence; but do ask for anything at all and we will aim to deliver.

Leave your woes at the door unless for some reason – and there are always exceptions – there is something that happens where family simply must come first. (At this point I would explain that I would always want people to be loyal and dedicated but in return I would remain flexible and would always accept reasonable explanations for time-off requirements in exceptional circumstances. Why other small business owners do not set this as their standard, I do not understand.)

Mistakes will be supported, indeed we positively encourage the concept of every individual trying and testing the current standard. We do insist that when mistakes are made people own up and aim to learn from the experience and share these learnings, plus there is no such thing as 'it is not my job' in our company.

It is always OK to question anything – but on the condition that the individual with the concern has a suggested solution as to how the problem might be tackled better.

Finally, treat the company and its belongings as your own. (I remember the pain of having to personally fix my own fax machine in the early days and valued the investments we made in all sorts of electronic everything. I would explain that we were a frugal bunch and also that I expected everyone to muck in.)

There are lots of other bits and pieces that I am certain I threw into what I always aimed to be an inspiring, entertaining conversation – one where, more than anything, I wanted to get across the approachability and the open nature of the company. Plus, of course, the message that the company expected the very best, pushed individuals hard and expected in return to give great opportunities and education. I felt that being honest about the ferocious pace of the Pacific day was something that would sort the wheat from the chaff – and my goodness, did it. We learnt within days whether a new recruit was going to make the grade or not. It took me time to appreciate quite how different a working day at Pacific Direct was for some people, but we never misled anyone and always made the demands clear from the outset. We also always worked hard to balance the demands with the potential rewards.

Ground rules

The Pacific Direct team devised ground rules and practised them relentlessly, holding each other accountable. The power of this open ability to constructively challenge each other is another priceless piece in the puzzle of running a really happy workplace. Here are the team rules:

1. I will always be positive, professional and respectful of others.
2. I will always exceed customer expectations.
3. I will be more effective and efficient which will result in profit, personally and professionally.
4. I will admit and work to resolve and learn from my mistakes.
5. I will find someone to praise each day.
6. I will embrace the Pacific commitment to its 'Impact on Society'.

There are a million creative ways to create positive momentum and reasons to do things differently. I would suggest that in today's business you have all the potential in the world to make your workplace more entertaining, flexible and enjoyable in the name of staff retention than at any time in the past.

Twenty ways to motivate your staff (without paying them more!)

1. Recognise success...
2. and share mistakes.
3. Sort yourself out first (you do have to be self-disciplined and you have to lead by example).
4. Use consultants – with extreme caution.
5. Make employees into owners.
6. Invite your staff to board meetings.
7. Encourage a social life outside work.
8. Get rid of 'them and us'.
9. Always give choices.
10. Give them money – cash.
11. Competition is healthy – make the message clear.
12. Let them work when they want to.
13. Keep it simple.
14. Respect everyone's unique abilities.
15. If you must give a car, can you pool it?
16. Make them winners (you never need to own an idea).
17. Tell people what their benefits cost.
18. Set up a payroll giving scheme.
19. Give birthdays as holidays, perhaps, or encourage leaving early for special family events.
20. Give them security through open communication, honesty and fairness – all applied consistently.

The actual strategic value when I left Cranfield was merely paper and vision. At that time we had some brand partners, barely a defined licensing agreement and we were also only just emerging on a global platform with new customers. You could say I was talking the talk – in advance of delivering the promise. I did not see it like this at the time; my Cranfield learning had allowed me to review my endeavours, revise my plans, and refocus my energies to enable me to clearly communicate our direction and the changes we needed to undertake to get us to our goal.

During the course I had already made the decision to stop directly promoting our house-line sales (invented brands). Although I had not actually worked out quite how to maintain some of the revenue stream, we did have some ideas in this regard. I also clearly recognised that if we were to really be an interesting partner to global groups we would need to add to the brands we had in order to maintain a cutting edge and refreshing offering, and also to allow new opportunities and exclusive arrangements with the many premium hotels around the world.

It seemed common sense to me, having had feedback from the hotel market about their desires to be unique and outstanding, that the company with the wider brand offering and original product ranges would constantly remain appealing and attractive to the hoteliers who were always searching for the outstanding premium-perceived-value products. Hotels are terribly inter-competitive and watch each other like hawks in terms of the 'points of difference' they can market to attract the wealthiest clientele. You might be surprised to know that toiletries play a huge part in the level of guest satisfaction, and that hotels therefore spend a great deal of time and attention in selecting the appropriate product partners to complement their overall style offering and the statements they make to attract their customers. If everyone broke down their own offers in such a way as to understand exactly how their marketplace approached their product area, then perhaps business people would find it easier to establish an outstanding offer that would be constantly in demand.

Despite all the positivity and confidence of our new approach to the market, the workload I had to balance was immense. I think at that stage we were supplying nearly a hundred countries all over the world and were learning all the nuances of importing into ports and places with unpronounceable names and dealing with people in far-flung places. I cannot underline enough the pleasure of working with many nationalities around the world. I do believe that we are all the richer for the experiences we gained and the information we shared in working in the hospitality industry, both within the Pacific family and those that we encountered from the hotel world on all continents.

The bravery of making a unique offering and specialising in only licensed branded toiletries with an additional one stop shop for complementary accessories was not something I recognised as outstanding at the time. It was more of a protective niche strategy, allowing the big global players to fight for three- and four-star provision whilst we focused wholly on luxury. On listening to our customers, I very quickly refined the important points of my sales pitch and that of the training we gave internally so that every player in Pacific sang consistently off the same song sheet.

Developing culture, and company weekends away

Over the years we developed the brilliant and utterly priceless concept of a weekend away with the team. It was challenging to get the right balance between play and learning and, given that we continually had new members of the team, it was impossible to ensure that some of the longer term team members gained as much as new entrants. However, it was without doubt the simplest way to gain momentum, focus and buy-in to the year ahead goals and objectives for all. In general, I believe that any excuse for putting your team players together will benefit your company.

The company charity was another important part of our culture, and the process for selecting an annual charity soon became a firm fixture in the company weekend away. Nominations were presented by any staff member who felt they had a good cause for the year. These were presented in a five minute slot (which was usually tearful as people would always pick causes close to their own families), and then we would vote on them in the evening. This is a brilliant and fair way of getting everyone involved in the company to select a cause for the year, and for years we worked to give money and time to a number of worthy causes.

Raising money – for charity

One of the best ways we raised money was by auctioning skills. Every member of the team had skills they could sell, or time that could be auctioned in exchange for cash for the cause. Examples would be things like babysitting, chauffeuring people to the airport in the holiday season, or individual culinary skills such as a curry night or tapas delivery. One of the best was the 'sale' of tiling skills, and another was the offer of a massage from one of our team who was taking a course to become a professional masseuse.

I have thought about the simplest way to demonstrate the added value of culture in terms of actual shareholding profit, and here is my suggestion.

I believe that the majority of Pacific Direct team members in the UK alone worked an extra five hours a week (this is a very conservative figure). They often worked through lunch breaks, which should not be ignored, turned up ridiculously early for work, set off outrageously early for travel – and sometimes travelled on a Saturday so as to save money through cheaper international travel fares. People often worked late, took work home, continually worked whilst travelling and went without sleep on journeys, putting up with me discussing potential. We ate together often – and the price of a meal is a small price to pay for the feedback you can gain during all types of company meetings.

- So, to quantify this, take five hours extra from people enjoying the workplace: 5 x 30 people (United Kingdom only), x 253 working days = 37,950 hours a year.
- Dividing that lot by a working week of 48 hours gives 790 more weeks worked in a year.
- And dividing that by 52 weeks equals 15 more members of staff for the team effort as a whole.

There were, of course, some challenges created by the power of our culture but none that in any way really dented our potential. The fact is that new team members were vetted and approved for recruitment by those who were going to work with them, and this drove higher standards of recruits who came into the company with clear expectations. We used to have a saying that if anyone survived induction and more than a few weeks without showing any signs of wobbling, then they were a good 'un and highly likely to stay the course. We did have a defined induction process, and you can find an example at www.companyshortcuts.com/documents.

I appreciate that some people will challenge the expectation I held that people who joined Pacific should and would willingly expect to work harder than they would in average companies.

During the recruitment process we were always very clear about the demanding workplace, the unacceptability of standing still in a role and the importance of training and education both internally and externally. In return for the demand I placed on everyone, Pacific could afford to celebrate in more original ways, and do so more regularly, whilst maintaining an enjoyable working environment and momentum. It was not always possible to be like this. Business potential and profit always dictated what we could and could not afford. Nevertheless we tried always to be fair and clear about expectations – in doing this I am proud to say I only ever had one complaint about our approach to people and that was that we gave them too many flowers (I will let this one stand)!

Developing people

Dealing with people challenges (giving feedback) is a much-underrated skill that has to be practised, trained and embedded in a company culture. There should never be a time when feedback cannot be appropriately communicated.

Feedback

- Start with asking an individual how they think they are doing.
- Ask for a suggestion on what might be improved.
- Share the expectation that improvement is required and that a better outcome is expected (to the extent that it is relevant).
- Encourage the potential for change and find out if there are any barriers to doing so that can be removed.
- Agree that a new way forward should be applied and move on with a constructive and planned process.

An ability to always demand the best from others can only, I think, be sought if you apply the same approach to yourself. A no-surprises culture of frank honesty will allow a company to accelerate past those businesses without one. As an aside here, let me add this: don't bear grudges. Following through on any commitment to an individual will make or break a relationship. Always put staff matters first, and sort them out fast and with clear decision and consistency of behaviour in all dilemmas.

You do have to work relentlessly at 'culture' and I would suggest that this is an area of the company that you can never quite let go. You will need to motivate and reward your direct reports, even at a time when they are the ones caring for the company's cultural momentum in the business as a whole. I could not count how many large bunches of flowers or good bottles of booze we gave out at Pacific to congratulate, recognise or thank individuals. If someone has achieved something worthwhile and you wish to praise, then don't skimp – make the gift impressive and meaningful; after all you are sending out a message to everyone else in the business. There are times when generosity in such matters is an investment in your asset as a whole. Big bouquets of flowers that last make an impact and motivate others.

Infectious desire to share success should be a foundation you protect. It is difficult to maintain as a company grows, but with a divisional approach and good management, clear rewards systems and the freedom to use authority, each leader in your company should be made aware that they are responsible for the culture as a whole as part of their daily approach.

Another way to retain culture as you grow is to make the effort to share what works with managers, assume that they need to learn how to create culture, and spend time teaching them how. Share what has worked elsewhere and let them add their ideas for a particular country approach and see how it goes. We did some awesome development of individuals running company weekends away in the USA, China and the Czech Republic – where they met with a fantastic response.

Adding value to individual development

We did many things to add value to people's development at Pacific in addition to the weekends away. Read through these twelve points which cover some of the most basic ones, and see what you could add to your own business.

1. Recruitment was, from the outset, based on a clearly defined role and this was shared with other people whenever relevant. I have never understood the method of allowing a new recruit to literally 'turn up' for a new job without a planned introduction and some earlier exposure to the team they will be working with. It is divisive, lacks constructive potential and minimises chance of success. Arrival was followed by a thoroughly planned and all-encompassing induction process (including all players) to allow exposure to all the parts of the business.

2. Genuine bi-annual career development reviews.

3. Key Performance Indicators (KPIs) with SMART goals. These were measured jointly at the year start to allow clarity for each individual on the way forward and their piece in the puzzle. In addition, we shared the company annual goals and targets.

4. An 'ask and ye shall receive' culture. Everyone knew the rule at Pacific regarding applications for spending money on training. If an individual could present a good enough case for attending a course, explain the benefits to them personally and the expected value to the company then we would support any suggestions.

5. We did not hire consultants at great expense. Indeed, I hardly ever used consultants as I always felt we had better people in-house who could learn from a 'challenging project' – perhaps not always their belief at the outset. If you do this you will be constantly amazed by the results delivered by anyone who is set a challenge and instilled with support, belief and a respect that they will get the job done. Sometimes a project approach with set parameters is a way of testing someone's willingness to grow – and you may find a possible bonus a great way of getting more hours out of individuals who are showing willing and looking for more.

6. Down-to-earth common sense applied to personal challenges that individually arise is the backbone of success, but do not take precedence-setting lightly. Everyone should be treated equally and no one should be forced to join in events; it does your culture no good and not every person is the same.

7. We ensured that management knew the rules and were given enough leeway to develop their own success and celebrate, with their own budget to spend on their teams. If you do not do this you cannot expect your own personal efforts to filter through as the organisation grows. Your management have to be employed – or, better still, promoted internally – with clearly defined expectations for getting a job done. The longer you maintain speed of decision-making and flexibility in

meeting a client's needs, the more powerfully your growth will be maintained. Your own personal leadership behaviour is fundamental to those around you, so be consistent at all times. And be big enough to apologise if your behaviour gives the wrong impression.

8. Results were shared openly through monthly team briefings. These provided all players with priceless open communication on the progression of the company. I cannot emphasise enough the value of such events, which we held around the world, and the added momentum these opportunities gave the business as a whole.

9. Equality and trust were given unreservedly but within clear conditions of culture. The non-hierarchical environment we fostered enabled input from everyone; we heartily encouraged new joiners to bring their ideas, knowledge and experience to the company. Seeing the way 'others' approach their businesses can bring massive value, and at one stage we were great supporters of the 'best in practice' shared exposure to some really cool companies which team members visited.

10. People exchanged skills so roles could be covered comfortably during holidays.

11. We had impromptu breakout updates on exciting events or significant changes in the business.

12. And we had 'down the pub evenings', which can be priceless, not least in emphasising the importance of down time out of the office for all employees.

We also introduced 360-degree feedback, which proved very powerful. Admittedly, the thought of sitting in a room surrounded by your employees giving you feedback about your behaviour, approach or indeed anything is hideous. However, I learnt a great deal from this process and hope I had enough humility to learn from others. This is not terribly British, and is somewhat pointless if the culture of the business is not one that is open and constructively looking for continual improvement. Despite the obvious discomfort of being a lot less than perfect, I felt that it was only fair, given the feedback I gave and the drive I displayed, to expect others to treat me in the same way as I treated them. My team taught me a great deal about how not to behave and I hope, over several years of practice, I nearly became quite a decent human being. You cannot expect someone to change unless they are given constructive criticism about their poor performance.

Celebrating success – ideas and inspiration

- One of the best celebrations that we gave at Pacific, and one which I know is still greatly valued today, was the time we had a professional photographer come to the offices for a day to take pictures of each member of the team – with anyone they invited to be in their shot. Family portraits were taken, as were team pictures and all sorts of variations on the theme. This was an especially good gift for a small company where many individuals could not afford the luxury of professional photographs, and the end result was a treasured gift.

- On moving offices to our biggest and most professional base we held an opening event for suppliers and customers, staff members, their families and any other professionals who were involved. We had magicians and cartoonists attend, and I found the warmth and environment these opportunities created was resounding.

■ Inter-company competitions took the tedium out of long days. They were small events – such as a dance competition – we held to change the workplace. We often made money for local community charities in the process and always laughed a lot.

And celebrations were not confined to the employees:

■ When Pacific raised its 10,000th invoice I was formally presented with a copy. I had no idea at the time quite how many customers we delivered to but the surprise was priceless in giving me, and other team players, a boost in knowing quite how far we had come.

■ At our tenth anniversary I was presented with a custom-designed graphic carefully framed in memory of some of the 'house custom invented' brands we had developed and then killed. As a reminder of the brave strategic decision we made to drop these brands and really focus on five-star luxury provision this piece is oddly meaningful, even today.

Leadership by example

I expected my senior team to treat others as they expected to be treated by me. For some the 'shockingly' open nature of our business took time to adapt to, but in the end they came to terms with it. 'Buddy lunches' were an example of such openness, and one you can put into practice easily. Get members of your team to have cross-over lunches on a regular basis with a member of the team whom they would normally barely be exposed to. The benefits run both ways, of course.

As a business leader you are likely to have loads of experience and knowledge you can share to the benefit of your team, and all it will cost you is time. Time spent in the short term will reap rewards from a better-educated and motivated group in the longer term. An example of this is learning how to read (that is, translate from legalese) a contract/brand licence translation/financial agreement. I used to talk through contract points with the sales force on new licences so that they were under no illusions about the performance promises that we had made and the seriousness of the commitment that brands made to Pacific by licensing us. I saw this as a trust given which needed to be repaid.

You will need a clear strategy – one which is simply defined and understood by all from the outset of their employment – to get the team on board in the whole ambition of the company. It needs to be communicated over and over again. Like a sales request, you need to keep repeating the message – not once, not twice, but over and over again. So can all of your team answer these questions: What is the purpose of the business? How does it make money?

Another powerful tool which can aid company momentum and knowledge, and set a great foundation as a business accelerates growth, is the time dedicated to competitor study. I cannot believe how few people believe that competitor study adds value. Perhaps I see this too simply. My competition wanted a bigger piece of my cake and I wanted to know how they thought they were going to get it. I wanted to beat them at everything they did; I wanted to be in growth markets before they were, to be recognised as the innovator and be more knowledgeable about the marketplace I competed in than they were. I never did much other than respect my competition and, with the exception of being sued by one of them in the USA, I was always open-minded about what I could learn from them in order to help Pacific's better progression.

How to do competitor research

We built a template around the knowledge that would help us to really get to know the key players in our market. To do this, roughly, assume you are writing a business plan on them: basic stuff like tracking their company accounts, recording any price detail on a central database that comes to you (oddly, in the old days this was sometimes faxed through by customers), and keeping an up to date SWOT analysis of their business is important. For me, dipping into competitor websites became an interesting pastime, as did collecting brochures, samples and measuring response times in service that would give us clarity about their operational efficiencies.

Check out your competitors at exhibitions and trade shows – and if you can drive by their offices, visit. And think about suppliers too; it was always interesting seeing a supplier making products on behalf of Pacific Direct's competitors: interesting to see what they were doing with their packaging, labelling; how they were managing their volumes. Simply asking a close supplier how much they are doing can also make you feel good.

I once devised an offer that every member of the company should book a hotel stay at Pacific Direct's expense to 'study' and learn about the hotel industry – and our competition. Undoubtedly the best way for us all to take a huge step in understanding the industry we served, the products we competed with and the challenges hotels faced was to expose all of our people to the actual environment in which our product ended, but with a challenge attached. Each person had to present all the items they had seen and could bring a sample of, or present anything they had learnt or experiences they had had from staying in their specific hotel. And, yes, I did choose the hotel list with specific competitive mixed focus in mind.

Employing people from within your own industry can be a huge leg up and is another way of assessing your competition. I have been known to interview someone with no real intention of employing them, just to gauge what kind of threat they might be, but in the end a really great member of the competition could easily be found a job if I was convinced enough of their skills. This particularly applied when opening in a new international market, where I almost always employed people with existing hospitality experience. They had a valuable head start in knowing people and being connected. However, generally treat industry recruits with suspicion; they carry knowledge that makes it easier for them to seem better than they are – something that is particularly true of sales types.

Motivation

Endless surveys show that social value factors are more and more important as people have choices in their job roles. Overwhelmingly people place higher importance on issues like having good management relationships; salary and benefits apparently come much further down a list of priorities. Community opportunities, learning, people preferring to be stimulated and challenged and needing to feel valued at work through having their contributions taken seriously and acted upon are more important.

The way one individual communicates and is heard by another is simply a priceless art that every manager should practise daily with listening and thinking skills. Your team need to know you believe in them. Trust them to push on, encourage them to actively look for improvement – and the better an individual gets as a business grows, the faster that organisation will have fall-back support.

Lara's laws

■ Work every day on your culture, the development of your people and the potential you can engender from trusting others.

■ Time taken to communicate focus, company strategy, expectations and results is simply priceless – and the return on investment is huge.

■ Employ 'smart and fast' – you will often get the best results from someone experienced, someone from within your industry, especially on the sales side.

■ Even if times are tough, there is still something happening, somewhere, to celebrate. Find it and build on new potential.

■ Competitor study should be planned into your week.

10
The Jelly Baby principle – strategies for success

Chapter goals

- Learn some basic business principles as early as you can, then apply them rigorously and change the focus of measure according to demand.
- Have a niche strategy to maximise your value and to help you stay under the radar as you grow and become world leading in your specialism. Reputation is powerful.
- Persistence and consistency in multiple ways remain key attributes; demonstrate them continually.
- Aim to create high barriers to entry in the offer you make. The customer lock-in value and the inability of competitors to copy what you do adds value.
- Licensing is a specialism you can teach yourself; check out www.companyshortcuts.com/documents.

Having studied the global market during my time at Cranfield, I was frightened of Pacific Direct being eaten up by mass global providers, companies offering low-cost products to major chains without actually listening to what their clients wanted.

I had come to understand what global hotel buyers wanted (unique, exclusive but recognised brands, at reasonable prices and in suitable packaging). I recognised the need to offer a globally safe, intelligently designed product, and one which came from a world class, customer services focused supply chain. The niche positioning to protect me from big competitors who focused on mass put me in line with the top of the hotel standard. These buyers wanted a single source to get the best price, without risk of product dilution through outsourcing, so we had to make the products ourselves. They also wanted advice, brand intelligence and a passion for finding the right products for their marketing needs, ones that would impress their demanding clients. There is little in business more powerful then selling a product that your client raves about. So does your strategy really meet the needs of your buyer? Is there a missing piece in the supply puzzle that concerns your client about the current marketplace offering, and which is a gap you can fill?

My vision was that we had tested the model of being a global provider, and we should therefore use that platform to massively grow our global provision of the full concept of guest amenities – as with the contract with Sofitel from September 2001.

I did not really like the phrase 'a one stop shop', which is often used in mass industry. Nevertheless, I could see the value of having a single supply chain source for all the hotel amenities; it would be highly attractive to brand marketers, marketing and procurement, as a reduced administration cost. The luxury industry needed to be able to understand what we offered as an original niche provider of fully coordinated, well-designed and competitively purchased items. I never claimed to be the cheapest in sourcing all the articles, but buyers could see that by consolidating purchasing, shipping, delivery drops and all the administration services of all the bedroom articles that we could source and often make in one country, the hidden savings were vast. The upside of supplying a broad range of products from a single source – with the clear strategic boundary that if someone wanted a product we could supply it – allowed us to beat the competition across a range of services and also made the possibility of us losing sizable contracts much more difficult. Once I had understood and could present the savings we could estimate on top of the way we could service properties on a global platform, we then only had to develop training material to support company-wide education on the complete and original offering we were taking to the market. These were exciting times for Pacific, and our next development stage focused on a strategic sales attack on core targets that we knew would benefit from our approach. I invented terminology for this which made it more memorable: Group Attack. There's another lesson here: give bold and inventive titles or easy-to-remember reference words to big projects that you wish people to grasp as being important, and keep repeating them.

As Pacific grew, I continually tracked the importance of significant global contracts. These would accelerate our number of customers much faster than hotel by hotel conversion and supply. Although individual, world-reputed hotels were hugely beneficial when we entered new markets, the scale of winning chain business with a central head-office instruction to use one of our brand ranges was immensely profitable in many ways.

I knew that given the success of Sofitel, there was little stopping the repetition of our offering to all the global chains. The problem I had was that the two factories Pacific Direct had were literally competing with each other and not playing on the same team. Why? Well, it took me too long to realise that although we were all part of the same company, I was never going to get them to bat for the same team because of the shareholding structure that we had – not without making structural changes to our set-up. We had to globalise our systems. And so a very painful set of steps started to take place.

I realised that the approach of our China General Manager had become a brake on our potential development, and we worked together towards a satisfactory conclusion to his tenure at Pacific. There is little more sensitive than the removal of a highly influential and experienced person from an operation. The deal you do when you sell or buy anything has to be fair to both parties, and this applies to many other scenarios. Often people refer to win–win situations – the objective, apparently, that both parties get an equal win of a particular deal. I think it is very rare that a genuine win–win occurs, but I can honestly say that I think in this situation the two of us struck a fair bargain. And considering the steep learning curve and the scale of work, the new Chinese team performed beyond any expectations. A 'similar but different' situation had also arisen in the Czech Republic, and again a successful deal was reached. This remotivated the country's General Manager and resulted in better performance as part of the group as a whole.

Strategy is destiny

I was still hungry for learning and, at hideous expense, I attended a course in the USA at Stanford through the Entrepreneurs' Organisation. I felt that I needed to refresh my energy and keep up to date with new business developments, and the particular programme I selected was called 'Strategy is Destiny'. I felt very excited to attend one of the great business schools in the world, but I was scared witless by the size of the huge pile of books I found in my room after I checked in. The quality of the course was fantastically engaging and, as always, I was able to learn as much from other attendees as from the lecturers. I worked exceptionally hard for a week as we studied recent success and failure stories of well-known organisations so that we could take away as much understanding as possible around the value of strategy.

Where are you going?

My ongoing plan for achieving sustainable growth was 'so far so good'. Check out these ideas and see if they can be applied to your own organisation:

Know the objectives of your business, ensure everyone else in your business understands them – and also really understands what the commercialism of making money in your business actually is. You may be amazed at how few people actually know how the money is made.

■ Ensure your objectives are measurable.

■ Has the route to achieving them been planned?

■ Have you shared your goals, and do you have an understood time frame for reaching them?

Know your competition.

■ Look at your successful competitors. Look for areas where your strengths overcome their offerings and exploit this message in the market. Be well respected and known in your industry.

■ Copy and improve on your competition's successful strategies.

■ Be knowledgeable and speak with authority – give solid factual advice and do not sell without utter credibility.

Communicate the expansion strategy to the business:
- Be clear.
- Be focused.
- Stick to your knitting.

Spend on the structure of the business, in these areas:
- Systems and technology.
- Marketing.
- Integrated process management for maximum efficiencies.
- Documentation to give education, guidance and short-cuts, and to maintain tried and tested processes.

Show how the business works:
- Monthly achievement records are shared.
- Consistency in management reporting.
- Measurements and dates give value impact to the business.

Be proactive:
- Get assistance and advice from those with experience.
- Ask the competition for help and/or shared knowledge.
- Meet the competition to SWOT the new players and new markets.
- Learn any technical language appropriate to your market.
- Read the trade press – know the market trends and general information.

Be predictable and consistent:
- In what you do.
- In how you do it.
- In where you do it and who you partner with.

Invest and share:

- Focus on sharing global knowledge.
- Use an intranet to avoid duplication if possible, and in the worst case have a shared, sensible and managed central drive where all the core documentation of the business is held – and make sure it is fully password-protected.
- Embrace any worldwide knowledge and expertise which is available.
- Love the business – do not depend on anything except the need to improve.

Continual growth is an expected part of any daily business. Standing still is never an option and the only consistent thing is change, so learn to embrace and run with it.

By the end of 2003 Pacific was lean and running well. Growth was huge, the opportunities for additions to the Brand Boutique were growing more and becoming more powerful and the methodology of getting bigger, and bigger-brand, globally recognised partners was improving with every pitch. I was in America the day I knew we had really cracked the brand impression and reputation we had worked hard to create. I was called directly by the person controlling the hotel amenities development of Bulgari – and his opening pitch was that he needed representation for his brand licence in the USA.

What took us to this opportunity was a series of developments which I think perfectly demonstrate the power of persistence in an approach. The reason I developed the Brand Boutique was that I saw Molton Brown charging a price for guest amenities that I could not charge for an invented brand. My first 'real' credible retail brand licence was with Neutrogena, but there were others before that, ones that helped get Neutrogena under

Johnson & Johnson to license me. I had been so excited by the Neutrogena opportunity that I felt we had to treat the brand differently, with greater investment. We presented Neutrogena in its own custom toiletries pouch and took a much more considered, luxury-focused approach to how we would mail out and sample potential clients with the brand.

As we gained one brand after another – and indeed one different brand serving a different part of the marketplace – we diligently managed the Brand Boutique so that we always respected the brand space in which any player targeted their consumer. For example I would sometimes turn down a brand license that someone kindly approached us to represent if the product looked to compete with a range we already represented or, more importantly, could preclude us from winning a brand we were actively seeking out – who we felt fit a hotel contract we were targeting. The right product mix for the gap client is smart marketing. If you are managing brand licences (or such a range of nearly competing products), the knowledge you must work to build on each brand, its placement and intentions will be critical to your future success. Building brand recognition is a double-edged sword and one to be very careful of. Initially you might beg for a brand licence relationship but then, depending on both your company and your brand's retail performance, that relationship demand can change dramatically. It can leave you – potentially – with some serious inconveniences, like stock-holding costs, the drain on your time, stressful misunderstandings and unnecessary meetings, with the long-term risk of damaged credibility which is vital in licensing. It's also a distraction from focusing on business growth and development – so it's a very expensive pastime and one to be avoided.

The important learning point of this whole process, all the way to when we sold the company, is that Pacific Direct always valued both the hand that paid them (the hotel customer) whilst equally appreciating the reasoning and value that a licence played for the brand owner in terms of risk and reward. The luxury branded licensed hotel amenities area remained a massive opportunity for exposure (in fact the market actually incorporates floating beds, in the shape of cruise liners, and also flying beds, in the shape of airlines offering in-flight kits to business travellers). The respect of both parties and the knowledge transfer between meeting the needs of both was critical if a brand was to remain satisfied with their exposure and level of trial, and if a hotel was to remain happy with their purchase and partnership of that brand and what the brand represented. Managing this relationship from the middle did bring some interesting challenges and, as in all markets at different times in the brand launch cycle, the value of the relationship to all parties would change. In any sales and service relationship you must work tirelessly to know where you stand in the cycle. You can then use this knowledge to your benefit.

Let's look at an example from my area of expertise. A luxury spa brand is coming to market but needs global expansion and reputation build in a particular market. If you can offer that exposure in the right luxury environment you have a powerful offer to make – and the licensing fee will not be as high as when the brand is established in the market. So...

- Strategic management understanding is critical.
- Follow the logic – if it feels right.
- Plan to plan, make the offer scalable.
- A niche approach is value added and allows premium positioning.
- Define it to your team and keep defining it to your customer.
- Build a diagram that simply details what you do and describes your market, and understand where your competition sits.

- Know and keep knowing your market.
- Goals, goals and more goals (measure everything and then decide what should be reviewed to check your course).
- Prioritise your time relentlessly – act with intent.
- Be utterly focused about your intentions and learn to say 'no' bravely to a brand licensing partner as you establish your line of expertise. It will increase your chance of succeeding with the partner and build your long-term credibility.
- Mission buy-in.
- Rewrite your plan regularly.
- Keep the right people; obtain commitment, expect them to filter down and share their expertise in exchange for skill development and investment in their own education.
- Continually align both teams with your objectives.

The fact is that it took me years to capture information professionally, with structure, continuity and in a reporting method that could easily be applied by all – but at least I got there in the end. One of the things I did to really hit home the message that I expected other people to lead, make decisions, be empowered and add value to the whole of the company was to run a series of management meetings, including all the senior management from each of the global divisions, to present on the same core details for their markets with the same level of detail.

From about 2003, when we started really applying this approach, we also started to really work as a unit. Knowledge of the global marketplace became more cohesive, the information on facts and figures was showing trends so we could really get under the numbers and understand how things were progressing. We also learnt more from each other about the strengths and weaknesses and needs of each business, which again allowed us to understand strategically what our possibilities were and what our priorities should be.

Make mistakes – and don't forget the Jelly Babies

I do still find it remarkable, given the endless mistakes I made, that it all turned out right in the end. Every business makes mistakes, and I am evidence for the fact that mistakes are not – usually – fatal. On the contrary, they can enable alternative direction and progress. Here are some examples of mistakes from my experience.

- Over-diversification. Being all things to all men meant we were masters of none, and I now utterly believe in having a niche focus.

- Stock overload. This led to chaos and profit wasted through both the cost of pallet storage space and wasted goods due to non-sales and 'best before' batch date destruction costs.

- Skill set sinking. As the company grew in the middle phase I started to lose my self-confidence – I cannot remember why – so I went through a phase where I started to recruit more qualified people as a priority over them having the right attitude, thinking that I could change their attitude. This is quite wrong. Employ people for the fit of their attitude and the aptitude can be taught.

- Being untargeted. Get targets in early, advertise them, stick to them and measure success.

- 'In, not on.' Everyone goes through the phase of thinking that their business needs their expertise on a daily basis – being continually available and endlessly involved, with fingers in every pie – and I was no different. How wrong was I? The sooner I learnt not to meddle, learnt to accept that others' methods might not be mine but might be even more successful and competent, and the sooner I stopped playing the problem solver and encouraged others to make their own decisions, the faster the business flew.

- Getting prioritisation wrong. The difference between the urgent and important and the important and non-urgent is vast, and I wasted a lot of time doing things in the wrong order. Relentlessly review what needs to get done, leading to the best return on investment of your time and effort.

- Having no barriers to entry. Every business has to learn to say no to business that does not fit their profit strategy and business focus, and we had to devise our own barriers to enable us to stay on focus. We introduced a system that allowed sales people to understand when to turn down client requests so that our team was not distracted following up enquiries that were not going to add long-term value for the company as a whole. We ensured that we could sometimes take on new projects that would potentially be exceptions to the rule, as sometimes a business has to catch a sprat to catch a mackerel. Many companies, though, make repeated mistakes by following business that is costing them resources and also exhausting a team by dragging them on chases that do not necessarily gain the results that are required for the overall objectives. Train people on how to turn business down in the right way (you will find this a difficult process to introduce only if you are far off the tracks in terms of process and clear commercial understanding). Adding these skills to everyone in your business through constant skills training and communication will build your potential. How often do you run internal training systems for the development of your staff?

■ Investing too little in marketing. This is a common mistake, but when correcting it do make sure quality rules apply and there is overall consistency.

■ Failing to network. Don't fall into this trap just because you are busy. You'll find more suggestions in chapter 7.

And finally, do remember to consider your employees. Without people, you have nothing, and forgetting that fact is a major mistake. Continual improvement processes will pay off if they are celebrated as standard. You must lay down in your business clear expectations of what you particularly value in your team of employees. Having an ambition to continually challenge the status quo will bring positive steps, both small and large, towards making greater profits or bringing in better opportunities that eventually bring better profits. Share your ideas and endlessly encourage others to share theirs, and you will be endlessly rewarded and energised by the brilliance of those you have around you.

With staff you reap what you sow, or so I believe, and I looked to celebrate every triumph. Rewards I have given have ranged from the smallest gift – a card saying thank you, a packet of Jelly Babies for a known Jelly Baby addict, tickets to the Chelsea Flower Show for a keen gardener – to taking the entire staff on holiday to Barbados for a week. Celebrate in style, whether small or large; it all counts.

Lara's laws

- Keep things simple, title them engagingly and repeat until the language you have used is played back to you – at which point, continue to repeat it with the same focused intent.
- Trust, encourage and celebrate your team.
- Bind clients into longer-term relationships which benefit you both by clearly outlining, succinctly and directly, the value you provide.
- Licensing is a promise you make based on your expertise in a market, and in which your brand partner sees value. Commit consistently and stick by your experience, or else you will create commercial nightmares.

11
Cut yourself some slack

Chapter goals

- Self-motivation and drive are key. How do you keep going?
- Reporting with facts, not noise, makes for great decision-making.
- Learn how to trust others to be accountable.
- Plan the life you wish to lead.

Not every day at Pacific Direct was an idyllic bed of roses for me. I constantly had self-doubt; I questioned every decision I made internally and I relentlessly doubted my ability and my luck throughout the time I built the business. I still feel charmed that we managed to create a global brand. Did I have intentions at the outset to 'have it all'? No – but I do know that anyone can do it.

Some say that 'having it all' is not as easy for a woman as it is for a man. In some ways I would agree, but I believe a balance can be established in leveraging the hell out of the advantage of being in the minority. You will need an awesome partner – here I was very lucky with Charlie – and may I remind you of the importance of physical fitness, and having drive like no other person you know. Many things will not go according to plan, but as long as you pick yourself up and have a Plan B, you can carry on.

The language of success, clear presentation of the company's intentions – my favourite word remains 'profit' – and the mission of the business as a whole have to be relentlessly represented throughout an organisation. A business owner has to be utterly passionate about what they are doing, why they are doing it and the intentions they have. (Incidentally, throughout my ownership of Pacific anyone who asked me whether I would sell got the same response. I ran the company to be the best we could be.)

By 2003 we had changed significantly as a business and were finding the international integration of the methods we applied quite a challenge. Leaders in these businesses had different management styles, for example. In the USA we had encountered terrific change in what I saw as a vital strategic market – one we had to conquer as 54 per cent of the leading luxury hotel owners have decision-makers based in the States. In fact, in our industry we could not be taken seriously unless we serviced the USA. In retrospect we perhaps entered the market too early, but we have never looked back.

Life planning

As I've said, I learnt a great deal from an organisation in the UK called the Entrepreneurs Organisation. Through the EO, I attended a lecture on life planning and then applied the same lecture (as best as I could) to those in the company. It is not easy to have it all – and although I believe entrepreneurs can be taught, I also believe that certain characteristics have to be inbuilt. The only person in charge of your own success is you. I was brought up to take responsibility for my own actions; I was given the chance to build my own self-confidence; I was given a lot of independence. I learnt to overcome obstacles and I learnt to be organised. From early on I developed my own determination to do things and go places. Decision-making has not been a problem since, and is an absolute necessity when running your own show. Weigh up the pros and cons, make a decision, act and move on according to the consequences. Too many procrastinators talk a good game but you cannot progress without action.

As a wife and mother I know what I like doing and what I do not like doing, as anyone does, of course – but I worked out the value of my time and energy in different areas and I constantly review and access the balance of these hours and days. I often get things wrong. I do not believe balance is impossible but I do know it is impossibly difficult to achieve and is always a passing moment. I also fully recognise that I perform better – with total engagement of my attention and interest – with little children in small doses and that I find it entirely unfulfilling to be a full-time mother. Not that I do not admire those that do a far better full-time job than I have ever tried to do, but for me it was always better to spend quality time with my children, rather than lots of time being miserably torn from my first 'child': Pacific Direct. Some of the things I did to achieve a certain goal may seem ludicrous but given the hours of the day, the ambitions of being both a mother and a business leader have meant I have had to adapt accordingly. I have also asked others around me to adapt with me.

Here are some of the things I have found to be most helpful:

■ Be organised and effective – you can learn to hone these skills through practising established techniques. I mentioned *The Organised Executive* in the previous chapter; try getting a copy and applying its lessons.

■ If you also have children, get a world-class nanny and treat her as such – especially if you are a woman. That person will be core to your success and give you the freedom to achieve every other possibility.

■ Plan your diary in advance – relentlessly – and share this plan with your support network on a regular basis.

■ Have holidays – real ones – and allow others in your business to truly be in charge – and accountable. At this point I would like to share a little bit of my frustration around entrepreneurs' approach to holidays. In the early days, the harder you work, the faster your venture will get past the break-even point, and then you will deserve a break; not before. But once you are capable of having a holiday, have a *real* holiday. Set ground rules, with a really capable person running the show and being your only means of contact, and then expect not to be interrupted. Plus, when you book a break, be fair to your team. Let them know well in advance, initially select those times of the year when nightmarish problems are less likely to arise, and then trust in the abilities of your team to protect your private time – as you will protect theirs. You should never, *ever* expect your team members to be in touch during their own breaks.

■ Treat yourself when you really need to.

■ Use the hours of the day to your benefit and apply yourself in such a way that you manage your peaks and troughs in performance because you might be pushing the boundaries. (For example, I work best in the mornings – indeed, I often achieved more by 9 a.m. than many people did in a day.)

Back to the business...

By the time 2004 arrived Pacific Direct had weathered a very tough period, and not just as a result of the impact of 9/11, SARS and foot and mouth; the Asian hospitality markets had also been damaged and Middle Eastern growth had been devastated. A business should always be able to handle market downturns to the value of 20 per cent of turnover – but these relentless demands were far more severe.

The difficult times we had been through gave us endless challenges – but also some opportunities. Irrespective of this I was feeling very low and starting to feel overwhelmed by the emotional strain of always putting my best foot forward with a smile on my face; on a personal level, I had by now had my third child and had dealt with the emotional and structural hurt of a one-third reduction of the Pacific team. There had also been two hard years of driving Pacific Direct through its biggest global launch. Although we were finally weathering the after-effects of September 11, I was exhausted.

At this point I concluded that I no longer enjoyed the instability of the hospitality market, irrespective of our continued profitable growth. I felt that it was time I sold the company and let someone else do a better job. I decided that the momentum coming from the Brand Boutique would make Pacific Direct a highly attractive acquisition, and felt that on a trade-sale basis there would be a great deal of interest (though there were some times in the days running up to this decision where frankly I considered giving away the company for 50 pence). We went through the hideous preparation of an information memorandum – a company sale document – which we presented to a number of suitors, and we nearly sold for £9.2 million pounds. How glad am I that the sale fell through, as Pacific Direct sold a few years later for more than double that amount.

Every decision I took from that point onwards was, however, made with full awareness of my next planned exit attempt. I learnt lessons from the failed sale, and put a huge effort into letting go and allowing a great management team to develop and step up. At this point I would suggest that once you are running a business, run it as if you might need to sell it that very day. Keep your paperwork in such a condition that you are always able to focus on the deal for the business sale and not on the paper jungle demanded during due diligence, which is both distracting and exhaustingly tedious. Get yourself a space in a virtual data-room and put any of the necessary documentation you will need safely in these folders. This will also help if you are thinking about making an acquisition.

For myself, I took a three-week break and returned to fight another day. I ran the Chicago marathon in 2005 as a method of rebuilding my self-confidence and also because I had started to live a little more. I had a reasonable management team, capably led by Rachel Groom, and we were starting to see a second tier of management develop in the company. We introduced the perfect monthly report, one showing the least profitable clients – thus allowing us to cull, change contracts or give notice where necessary. You must, as a business, know who makes you money, in priority order, and who is losing you money, and this is not always obvious in the numbers. Another excellent report was regional profitability. This clarified the sales position. Some sales people believed that their regions were the most profitable but, when actually analysed, the situation could be very different; due to the extra costs of some regional demands, their region could be much less successful than outwardly perceived. Learn from this; look closely, allocate costs appropriately and do not be afraid to share such valuable facts (and this report was also priceless when doing development reviews – including salary).

In 2006, having built the leading luxury brand proposition to the global hotel chains, we set about consolidating our position and building on an already substantial global platform for supply. It has been a massive privilege

In 2006 we were genuinely recognised as the leader in luxury guest amenities brand licensing and were literally turning down brand propositions every week. What an honour that companies worldwide consider Pacific Direct the company to represent their brand in miniature. The scale and reach of what we could achieve as a brand sampling exercise was immense. Indeed I remain surprised that some brands have never quite grasped the power of placing a product for trial – at the right level of target audience – where there is not other choice of product.

Pacific Direct started working with all of the leading luxury hotel chains and consortiums and we had the pleasure of working with some of the most talented hoteliers worldwide. Hotels constantly look for the points of unique experience to offer their guests. They think hard and work relentlessly to achieve customer satisfaction – something we too had always put at the heart of our methodology.

Around this time I was thrilled to work with some of the leading cosmetics and toiletries companies in the world. I still pinched myself when having a meeting with some of the global giants but for a long time we had worked to perfect our processes and we built confidence as we continued to build on our capabilities. Having the giants in the toiletries and cosmetics world asking us advice on sampling was quite a defining moment for me personally – very rewarding.

Due to principles around the respect for the brand we represented, an intense knowledge of the hotels market and a clear mission committed to supplying only the best hotels Pacific had a momentum like never before. We would turn away brands of some considerable reputation if we felt what they expected was unachievable or simply because they had unrealistic commercial expectations. The lesson here is that if you simply cannot deliver a promise under a licensing agreement – don't license. Let me introduce you to a mantra which has helped me to expand my business in ways I'd never planned or even dreamed of: 'calculate your risks, and take them'. I do think some people are more naturally capable in this area – and I have also seen that without the ability to make decisions and act, progress is agonising.

Lara's laws

- Focus on one thing at a time, irrespective of all the other demands that come your way. Stay focused on that core deliverable.
- Look after yourself – small treats go a long way – and make the sacrifices worth it by measuring your success.
- Practise making decisions without procrastination, and do it enough to make it the norm.

Afterword – what next?

A life worth living, with love, laughter and learning as its cornerstones, is what makes me happy. The great big goal of many people is 'life balance'. What strikes me as strange is how many business leaders strive for this balance and, like many people, wonder why they are failing to achieve an all-round satisfaction with their lot. One great gift of having been fairly young when I started Pacific was the exposure to older statesmen at customer events and awards ceremonies. I cannot count how many times I was warned by successful business leaders not to make the mistakes they had made – principally missing out on the upbringing of their own children.

Many brilliant business leaders simply fail to plan their life, quite unlike the way they dedicate long hours and make massive sacrifices in order to make their businesses successful. Often people forget to apply the same rigorous dedication, self-discipline and ambition to having a wholly happy existence in other areas.

As I have said before, I cannot stress enough the importance of having a life plan of some kind. Whether it is shared or otherwise, writing down the things you want to achieve will be priceless. It cannot be said that everything will run smoothly throughout, but how you deal with the major events and challenges – going over, under, round or through hurdles – will be the making of you. Never take anything personally, never hold a grudge and always, always learn from your experiences. Learn constantly, admit when you are wrong, celebrate the brilliance of others and maximise the whole company's skills and abilities. Delegate as much as you can, measure relentlessly – and never, ever give up.

It can be lonely, and I would also advise having as many supporters as you can – and I recommend changing and outgrowing your mentors as your skills and the needs of your business change and progress. Another thing I did to fight the loneliness of being the leader was to take on public speaking engagements at which I could talk about Pacific Direct's success story. Oddly enough, these events added to my workload, were often unpaid, often held at inconvenient times and added to my already long days. But they rewarded me with the response I gained from sharing my challenges, mistakes and stories – a form of therapy, if you like.

Transition is a phrase coined for the time between selling one business and doing whatever comes next – for many, that is often another business. Believe it or not, transition can be a hideously lonely period for some people and there are only a few books to help them deal with the enormity of the challenge of selling a business, dealing with wealth for the first time (don't expect sympathy) and losing all the kudos that goes with being the leader in a demanding, vibrant and fast-growing organisation. I feel that the stage of a business when a leader is in the 'letting go' phase – really allowing others around them to make decisions, take actions and accountability – is the hardest phase for any previously wholly controlling entrepreneur.

Following the announcement of the sale of Pacific Direct pretty much everything carried on as normal from a work point of view, other than the odd press release and marketplace awareness; I stayed on for a year whilst the new management found a new CEO. For myself, I had a clear list of the things I wanted to catch up on and no other crystallised plans other than a passion for business – and for seeing others improve. One of my goals was to share the story of Pacific Direct, and I hope more than anything that I can encourage and inspire others that, despite all the challenges of running a small company, a business with people at its heart will maximise potential. It is hard work, but like most things that are hard-earned, it is well worth the reward.

What does success look like? For me it will be my new venture, Company Shortcuts. This will deliver a constantly revitalised information resource to small- to medium-sized business owners – resulting in better business performance, more employment opportunities and thereby a more stable community as a whole.

And you can help. I hope you have taken away bagloads of ideas, scribbles and actions to apply to your own company development. Please apply and see through the actions I have suggested to improve profit and company potential. Make time to plan and educate people – and yourself, of course – continuously. Please find a way to share the value of this story with ten other entrepreneurs like yourself, and please help me reach a million companies, impacting them in small and large ways to increase their overall success potential. Through mentoring others, having new courage through the tricks and tips I have shared, and applying the templates from Company Shortcuts, your contribution to this goal will give *you* payback.

The laws of lifetime growth

1. Always make your future bigger than your past.
2. Always make your learning greater than your experience.
3. Always make your contribution bigger than your reward.
4. Always make your performance greater than your applause.
5. Always make your gratitude greater than your success.
6. Always make your enjoyment greater than your effort.
7. Always make your cooperation greater than your status.
8. Always make your confidence greater than your comfort.
9. Always make your purpose greater than your money.
10. Always make your questions bigger than your answers.

I was given a copy of these some time ago, and was so impressed that I have carried them with me since. They come from *The Laws of Lifetime Growth* by Dan Sullivan and Catherine Nomura.

Appendix
Lara Morgan and Pacific Direct: major landmarks

1991: Started selling hotel amenities and had my breakthrough with the Dorchester.

1993: Jarvis Hotels, my first chain-hotel contract.

1995: I was voted Bedfordshire Businesswoman of the Year, which was a great accolade and gave me much-needed new confidence and momentum.

1996: Pacific Direct beat Coca-Cola as supplier of the year to my then favourite group of hotels, Jarvis Hotels. How cool was that – better than Coke!

1997: Buying the Czech business and establishing a factory in China – a busy year; we started our own manufacturing.

1998: The major licensing agreement with Neutrogena was really the first major brand-licensing step we achieved.

1999: Attending Cranfield's Business Growth Development Programme.

2000: Following completion of the Cranfield course, the PD team set a reward – that I should finance a Barbados trip in return for the company achieving £1 million profit in a single year.

2001: Company weekend away where we introduced the Golden Soap Awards. Everyone dressed in black tie and we celebrated the most successful performers of the previous year.

2003: The misery year of redundancies and 30% global staff reduction.

2004: I unsuccessfully tried to sell PD due to exhaustion, but took a break and regained my energy and focus. We met the £1 million target.

2005: Company week away in Barbados. This trip found its way into the *Daily Mail,* and people often remember Pacific because of this event.

2006: Further significant development in our Asian platform development.

2007: Serina Vong joined and became the backbone of our successful development in China.

2008: A major year for Pacific Direct as I sold my majority shareholding.

Index